SKY WAVES

SKY WAVES

The Incredible
Far East Broadcasting
Company Story

By

GLEASON H. LEDYARD

MOODY PRESS • *Chicago*

OTHER BOOKS BY THE AUTHOR

And to the Eskimos
Husky Talk
Arctic School Days
American Boys Sail Arctic Waters
Adrift on Hudson Bay

Printed in the United States of America

24665

*Dedicated to
the national workers—men and women—who
labor tirelessly in programming, studio work
and engineering. Missionary radio could not
be effective without their valuable help.*

The heavens declare the glory of God; and the firmament sheweth his handiwork.

Day unto day uttereth speech, and night unto night sheweth knowledge.

There is no speech nor language, where their voice is not heard.

Their line is gone out through all the earth,

And their words to the end of the world.

—Psalm 19:1-4

CONTENTS

7

FOREWORD

WHEN I READ Gleason H. Ledyard's book, *Sky Waves*, I felt as if I were reading a chapter added to the Book of Acts. The surprising succession of events that brought into being the Far East Broadcasting Company reminded me of the resurrection power of Christ.

This book is easy reading. Once you begin it, you will want to finish it. Throughout the entire story, the reader is carried along, wondering how God will work in one difficult situation after another, doing things which even the most dedicated Christian cannot do.

In this day of population explosion, an age-old message must be borne to the earth's millions through the most modern media. This is exactly what the men of the Far East Broadcasting Company have done.

I urge the reading of this book because I know that no person can remain the same afterward. Here is a story that smashes right through all the skepticism and secularism of our times and forces the reader to say, "Without God, things like this just don't happen!"

BILLY GRAHAM

PREFACE

To STAND ON THE GROUNDS of Christian Radio City in Manila makes one feel like Moses of old—God saying to him, "Put off thy shoes from off thy feet, for the place whereon thou standest is holy ground." To be electrified at the sight of white-hot filaments in the transmitter tubes; to gaze skyward into the maze of antenna wires and steel towers; to watch Filipino and American technicians work side by side; to stand on the shores of Okinawa in the shadow of KSBU's antenna array and to realize that of seven million Chinese bound in custody by Communism across the China Sea some are hearing the Gospel nightly; to see dedicated missionaries and nationals preparing programs in studios operated in Hong Kong, Viet Nam, Singapore, Thailand and India to be aired over FEBC's stations; to see the miracle station KGEI in San Francisco; to fellowship and share the burdens of consecrated staff members—these experiences and many more were the rare privileges of the author and his wife on a recent extended world tour.

These rich experiences, combined with the Far East Broadcasting Company's need for a written record of its incredible story (its beginnings as well as the way God has undertaken down through the years), resulted in this volume.

The author feels this preface should be in the form of an apology. After being challenged with what he saw overseas, he offered to undertake this writing. In a spirit of humility and with a very grave sense of responsibility, he started the work. Other efforts of writing done before were child's play compared to this undertaking. Previous books were writen from the author's own experiences and flowed from

11

his mind to the paper. However, this story was different. Reams of papers and letters had to be studied carefully. Back copies of the *Far East Broadcaster* were read and material cataloged. It wasn't long before the job looked overwhelming.

Several natural conditions have made the writing extremely difficult. Alternately, one or the other of the directors has spent six months in the Far East. The stories they told or put on recording tape have been either firsthand or secondhand accounts and there is a decided difference! In the first years, the records kept were not too accurate concerning minute facts which are important for a documentary record. What a perplexing problem to classify the power of certain transmitters! One time a transmitter would be listed as 2,000 watts. The next time it was mentioned, it would be 5,000 watts. Later 3,000 watts would be seen in some printed matter, and then 4,000 watts. All this time the author was listing these as separate transmitters, only to find in other material that the same transmitter was being referred to! Light finally dawned! The unit was homemade in the Philippines, and the engineer who built it probably overrated its capacity. The next engineer coming along said, "Why, that isn't 5,000 watts; it's closer to 3,000 watts." With constant modifications being made on the field, the home office actually didn't know at times what power they were using in Manila. (Evidently they didn't know themselves!) These conditions existed only in the early years. However, there were other problems.

Confusion of thought was dominant after two or three people told the same story. Prices, dates, watts, places, and numbers were often different. While driving to the FEBC office one morning, the author noticed a minor accident at the corner of Whittier and Washington Boulevards, within sight of the home office. At such a busy intersection and at that time of the morning, there were many witnesses. Without a doubt, if those witnesses would have been summoned to testify in court, few testimonies—if any—would have been identical. In fact, it could be presumed each testimony would present a different facet of the truth. Therefore, the reader can see how this narrative of FEBC might vary slightly from the story which could be related by some of the staff members—some who have come and gone through the years of FEBC's existence.

Unfortunately, not all the miraculous stories (or complete stories) can be told in a volume of this kind, because of the danger of implicating certain personalities and government officials.

Hundreds—yes, thousands—of letters have come to the hands of program personnel of FEBC stations, as well as missionary producers, in response to programs heard. Many of these are answers to requests for listener response with station-testing in mind. Others come from people, especially in some foreign lands, who enjoy writing letters and receiving replies. But the most important ones come from people who have been touched with the vital Message of Life. A very limited amount of these letters have been included in the pages of this volume—just a cross section. However, the reader should be cautioned that many of these letters came from poorly educated people or from those who had no education at all. Other letters were received from the educated class, and a high percentage were written in a foreign language and had to be translated into English by the local missionary.

In such translations, rich meaning and heart-warming expressions are often lost. Many letters written in English were poorly written with mistakes in grammar and spelling, but they were fragrant expressions of satisfaction in hearing the broadcasts. It is strongly suggested that the letters (which for the most part are unedited) be thoroughly digested to catch the full significance of how listeners are responding.

Grateful acknowledgment is made to Robert Bowman and William Roberts for their help in reiterating favorite stories that have been told many times in missionary meetings and conferences, also to Richard Bronson, who has been labeled FEBC's chief storyteller, and to Miss Terry Brennen for her work in typing the final manuscript.

It is the heartfelt desire of the author and the entire FEBC staff that Christians shall be challenged to hold the ministry of missionary radio before the Lord in daily prayer.

GLEASON H. LEDYARD

Chapter One

THE GENESIS OF FEBC

THE "BON HOMME RICHARD" had *just* catapulted her planes for a night mission. She was the only aircraft carrier for night torpedo and fighter squadrons in Task Force 38. The carrier had just left the main body of ships and was steaming along close to the Japanese mainland.

During the time the planes were away on their mission, the "Bon Homme Richard" ran into typhoon weather. Besides the inky blackness of the night, dense fog lay thick all around and fifty-miles-per-hour rain squalls lashed the flight deck. The huge carrier was being tossed about like a nut-shell. The planes were reported to be on their way back to the ship.

By shortwave communication and radar they were guided to the general vicinity of the carrier, but the fog was so thick the pilots could not see the carrier nor could the crew on the deck see the planes. Gas was running low; something had to be done! The crew were forced to try something that had never been tried or tested. They would attempt to guide the seven tons of metal coming in at one hundred miles per hour to that tiny speck on the Pacific—the flight deck of the "Bon Homme Richard"!

Watching by radar, the landing signal officer talked by radio to the pilot. The plane was guided down the side of the carrier some twelve hundred yards off to the port side. The pilot dropped his landing gear, flaps and tail hook. He was flying blind, depending entirely on the voice coming to him through the headphones. Then, as the radar indicated that the plane was opposite the stern, the word was given to

15

turn toward the carrier. Another turn brought the plane
astern of the ship. Still the pilot could not see the ship.
Every man on the flight deck that night held his breath and
strained his eyes to catch a glimpse of the plane coming in.
The landing signal officer and the pilot spotted each other at
the same instant. Frantically the officer gave a "cut" signal,
and the plane was jerked to a halt . . . as were all the others
that night.

Over on the superstructure of the "Bon Homme Richard"
stood a young warrant officer, John C. Broger. There was
something different about John from many of the men
aboard ship: he loved the Lord and desired to serve Him.
As the plane was being guided in by radio that dark night,
young Broger continually thought of Psalm 32:8: "I will
guide thee with mine eye."

This experience John had just seen confirmed something
he had been thinking about for a long time. Radio could
surely be used effectively in reaching the millions in Asia
with the Gospel of Christ. Not only did he have a technical
interest in radio; he was convinced radio had a future in
world evangelism.

* * * *

Nearly seven thousand miles east of where Broger was
stationed, Robert Bowman stood before a microphone in
studio A in the Haven of Rest Studios, Los Angeles. The
program: "Haven of Rest." "Bobbie," as he was then known,
was the second mate on the "Good Ship Grace," in this program heard daily on the Mutual system, West Coast Network, and once weekly, coast to coast.

As Bowman stood before the mike that day, his heart was
particularly warmed with the thought of some day being
able to use the miracle of radio in reaching millions in the
Orient. Such blessing had come to countless thousands of
people across America as the Word was given by First Mate
Bob (Paul Myers), while heart-searching messages in song

were sung by the Haven of Rest Quartet with baritone Bowman as soloist. God had been pressing this vision on his
heart for some time. Would the day soon come when transmitters could be placed on the other side of the Pacific and
the multitudes over there hear the Good News of Salvation?

* * * *

Pastor William J. Roberts had been in his study for several
hours working on the message for Sunday. Besides being the
pastor of a large church in the Los Angeles area, Roberts had
been on the air with a daily radio program, "The Family
Bible Hour." The Lord had been working in his heart in
recent months. He was reaching the people in his church
and he had a good listening audience on his program, but
God was laying a burden upon him to reach out farther than
just the Los Angeles area. And strangely enough, not
farther east—but to the Far East!

The war was fast drawing to a close. Activities were
tapering down in Europe, and it looked like some of the
theaters of war in the Pacific were under control. What was
on Pastor Roberts' mind that morning was the huge vacuum
caused by the aftermath of war. The millions that would be
hungry and homeless; the displaced persons; the many cults
rushing in to take advantage of the situation; the instability
of governments—these and many other thoughts were caus-
ing sermon preparation to drag a bit. If only radio could be
used to reach these countries with the Gospel!

Surprisingly enough, these three men were not total
strangers to each other—they were close friends. Many times
they had talked together about the possibilities of broadcasting the Gospel in the Orient. They prayed about it when
they happened to meet together, and as letters were passed
back and forth during those war years, comments were not
scarce about the possibilities of setting up a broadcasting
station some place in the Far East.

Word was received that the 38th Task Force Fleet would

be coming into San Francisco. Soon afterward John Broger
would be discharged.

Waiting on the dock were Mrs. Broger and the Bowmans.
Little time was wasted in getting together to discuss the
future. Night after night the three men talked and prayed.
Finally, it was settled; they would pool what money they
had—exactly $1,000.00—and form a nonprofit corporation.
On December 20, 1945, the incorporation papers were completed. They were in business!

They gratefully appreciated the lift First Mate Bob of
the "Haven of Rest" program gave them. He enclosed a
copy of the official organ of FEBC, the "Far East Broadcaster," in a letter to his mailing list. He offered to match
anything the men could raise; thus, receipt number one was
made out to "Haven of Rest" for $1,000.00.

Since Robert Bowman was well known to many people
across the United States, and Pastor Roberts was known in
the Los Angeles area, the Founding Fathers were far from
"unknowns," and Christians had confidence in them. Within three months $10,070.56 had come in toward the first
broadcasting station. The proposed amount needed—one
hundred thousand dollars!

Talk as you may on these shores, the problems of setting
up a radio station in a foreign land cannot be solved here.
Bowman was still with the "Haven of Rest" program; Roberts was still pastoring a church. Broger had an offer to enter business with a glassware concern, but the Lord indicated
differently.

Since John had just returned from the Far East, Dorothy
Broger was a bit reluctant to see her husband leave so soon
for another tour of duty—this time for the Lord in behalf of
finding a suitable place to establish the work of the Far
East Broadcasting Company.

Gathering on pier 55 at Wilmington Harbor, March 25,
1946, members of the FEBC staff and friends prayerfully

waved good-by to John Broger as he set sail for the Orient aboard an old freighter, the "Lane," a victory ship.

Many thoughts rushed through the minds of those standing there as the last bits of luggage were loaded and the last good-bys were said. In their minds they lived again those years in which God had been preparing the heart of each of them to carry out His purpose of preaching the Gospel to every kindred, tongue, people, and nation.

Again they relived the days of prayer and waiting upon the Lord preceding the incorporation of FEBC. After that the busy days of radio broadcasts and special services, setting up of the FEBC office, passport application, and finally, preparations for this journey itself tumbled through their minds in kaleidoscopic fashion.

As they stood there on the pier, it seemed as if they could see the turning of a new, fresh page in God's great plan for these latter days, for the very purpose of that journey into the Orient was to lay the foundation for the establishment of a radio transmitter which would carry the message of Christ's power to save to the millions of people in those Far Eastern lands who have never known the Saviour. Their hearts were raised in praise and thanksgiving that they were accounted worthy to have a part in the fulfillment of this great purpose.

"Bon voyage, John. The Lord be with you!"

Chapter Two

THE EXODUS

IT WAS A BIG DAY at the FEBC office when the phone rang and the operator said, "I have a cable for Far East Broadcasting Company. Shall I read it to you?"

"Yes, please!"

> "Arrived Shanghai safely. Lining up appointments. Pray."
>
> JOHN

On the other side of the Pacific, Broger had caught his first glimpse of the China coast. Arriving at the mouth of the Yangtze River, the ship lay at anchor for a day until a pilot took them up the twenty-five miles of river waterways to the sprawling city of Shanghai. In a letter dated April 19, he wrote:

> I am now staying at the China Inland Mission and recently had a long talk with James Taylor, grandson of Hudson Taylor. Tomorrow morning I have an appointment with Mr. Peng, who is private secretary to the mayor of Shanghai. He was formerly in the Ministry of Communications in Chungking, and in charge of the station there.
>
> . . . Prices here are out of this world. Exchange is $2,000.00 Chinese National currency to $1.00 U.S.! A meal is $2,000.00 to $3,000.00 and is about the size of a twenty-five-cent lunch in America. A pair of shoes are $1,000,000.00 or in U.S. currency $50.00. A 1940 Chevrolet is $10,000.00 U.S., and a white shirt is $35.00 U.S.!
>
> . . . It would be impossible to describe Shanghai in

these days. People are everywhere; the mass of humani-
ty is indescribable. Automobiles and rickshaws just
plow between them.

In another letter dated April 22, he added this note:

> . . . I can't get used to seeing dead children lying on
> the street. Yesterday morning I saw another dead baby.
> It was about one and a half years old and had all its
> clothes on and had just been put out with the garbage
> on the side of the street. The people are starving, both
> physically and spiritually.

During the days that followed, Broger had numerous
meetings with mission leaders and sought out every opportunity to learn of the possibility of establishing a broadcasting station on China soil.

On May 8 he wrote:

> . . . The sight of this land is enough to warrant the
> laying aside of all the comfort and ease in America.
> Just to walk down a little narrow dirty alley and see the
> mass of humanity—yes, even here in Shanghai, causes a
> great and heavy oppression to come over one. On every
> hand is death. In the temples of Hangchow I saw count-
> less numbers prostrate before immense golden gods,
> bowing their heads to the floor in vain hope that their
> crops might be watched for the coming year. So is the
> hope of the millions of China. How can we possibly
> live a life of ease and plenty when there is anything
> within our power that we might do to bring them the
> hope of Christ and His love?
> We have another member on our Advisory Board—
> James Hudson Taylor. He is head of the Northwest
> Bible Institute in Shensi Province. I have had fine fel-
> lowship with the Taylors. They are most interested in
> radio work. We meet together for prayer about this
> work every morning before breakfast.

As time went on, Broger had opposition in seeing about a franchise for a broadcasting station. The Nationalists were far from well organized. He was sent from office to office. No one would say "yes" and no one would say "no." The Nationalists, fearing the oncoming Communists, did not want to license a foreign group. Had they given Broger a franchise, they would have had to do likewise to Communist-inspired groups. The only commitment they would make verbally was that an application for 500-watt stations might be considered. But such a weak station for the millions of China would be useless.

One thing was certain—a recording studio was of utmost importance. And it needed to be set up as soon as possible to get some Chinese programming underway. Days were spent in trying to locate a suitable studio. With the complexity of such a city as Shanghai, and with a poor transit system, hours were consumed in trying to find addresses.

*   *   *   *

Back in America Robert Bowman was being led to make FEBC his fulltime job. He had spent over twelve years with the "Haven of Rest" broadcast, but now it was time to disembark from the "Good Ship Grace," and start an extensive ministry of meetings across the United States, at the same time keeping things in the office shipshape.

*   *   *   *

After many weeks of traveling and interviews with government officials, and the organization of the China Christian Broadcasting System, it appeared to be the proper time to make application to the National Chinese government for six 500-watt stations to be located in heavily populated areas. The newly formed Board of Directors, five outstanding Chinese laymen and clergy, were enthusiastically working together toward one goal—to send the Gospel out over the ether waves to the millions of Chinese.

In the meantime transcribing equipment* was being prepared in Los Angeles to send to Shanghai.

After six months of negotiations in China, John Broger embarked for Manila on a Chinese tramp freighter and bunked in the hold. Seeing people die on board was not uncommon. Until some firm action was taken by the National government on the request of the franchises, he felt it would be a good time to investigate the same possibilities in the Philippine Islands.

Arriving just two days after the country received its independence, he found Manila still in the midst of its celebrations. The unsightly sunken hulls of Japanese warships in Manila Bay were a grim reminder of the difficult war years. John started at once to set up a Filipino subsidiary of FEBC and probe the feasibility of a broadcasting station on Philippine soil.

Although Manila still had open sores from the war, the problems of meeting the right people to discuss broadcasting were not as great as had been the case in China. Attorney Leon O. Ty, outstanding newsman and publisher of the Philippines, befriended Broger and helped in opening the doors to high government officials. Broger filled out dozens of sheets of paper pertaining to the application and submitted them to the Minister of Communications. Within a few days he was called to the Radio Department office.

"Why didn't you fill in all the questions?" the one in charge asked.

"I just do not know some of the answers," John replied.

"For instance," the interrogator continued, "why didn't you state how you will be financed? And you didn't state the amount of power you will be using. And here is another one—you didn't give the location of the proposed transmitter site. We can't process this application unless *all* the

---

*This was back in the days before the advent of the modern tape recorder. Programming had to be done by cutting discs—or records.

questions are answered. So I guess it will have to be denied
on those grounds—unless you want to fill out new application
papers."

John left the office with new forms, a bit discouraged with
the work ahead of retyping all the material and trying to
satisfy the government with answers he didn't yet know.

Several days later he walked into the Radio Department
office with a lighter step in anticipation of the forms being
readily accepted. But the same questions were asked when
the Filipino behind the desk glanced at the three unan-
swered questions!

1. How will your proposed station be financed?
2. What is your proposed power?
3. Where will the transmitters be located?

John was a little red with embarrassment for not having
answered the questions as requested. But he didn't know the
answers!

"Sir, we have faith in God to meet our needs."

"Faith! What do you mean?"

"We believe God will supply all the money through dedicated Christians to build this station and keep it on the air.
We will not be receiving any money through advertising.
God will supply our needs," John returned, then quoted this
verse of Scripture: "Faith is the substance of things hoped
for, the evidence of things not seen."

"Well, I don't understand what that kind of faith is,
but if you think you can manage on that, we'll give you a
try. Now, about the power, how much?"

John's mind was whirling. He quickly said, "Ten thousand
watts," then held his breath! The man wrote in pencil the
words *ten thousand watts*.

"Where will your equipment be located?" he queried.

And that was where Broger was stumped. He couldn't
fish land out of the sky like he had just latched on to watts
of power!

"Could I have two days on that question?" he asked.

Leaving the office with determination to find a suitable piece of property, he contacted real estate men at once. This was not the first time he had thought of this. He had been looking for property for days, but skyrocketed prices were way out of reach.

Within six weeks an answer was received from the Minister of Communications. Broger quickly looked the papers over and his eye fell on one part. Someone had penciled out the words *ten thousand watts* and over top had written the words in large letters *Unlimited Power!* (So unorthodox was this that John could hardly believe his eyes.)

There was one condition, however: "Name the site where the station will be established." The paradox was that FEBC still had no land on which to build a station nor the kind of money it was going to take to buy acreage.

The "Go ahead" signal was given to the engineers to start building the transmitter at a concern in the midwest. It was impossible to purchase such items at the close of the war. Only the finest and most highly approved materials would be used. Areas to be reached with the shortwave transmitter were Dutch East Indies, French Indochina, Siam (as Thailand was then known), China, Russia, Korea, and Japan. The medium wave transmitter would be used for local broadcasting and would be first to be put into service. But where would they be located? That was the pressing question!

Broger, with members of the Philippine committee, searched day after day. Postwar prices were prohibitive. Because of the elaborate ground system of literally miles of copper wire that would have to be buried under the surface of the ground directly under the antenna towers (to help radiate the signal away from the ground) a parcel of ground would have to be hand-picked.

In a letter to the home office, John Broger said:

Let me say at the outset that living quarters are almost impossible to find in Manila and land is very expensive. When the permit was granted to FEBC, it was necessary to inform the government as to the exact future location of the transmitters and studios.

The answer to this problem was another of God's answers to prayer. Recent governmental regulations were such that our transmitter would have to be built so far away from the city of Manila that it would be difficult for missionaries to get from the city to the station. Then too, the prices of sufficient land for the station ranged from $40,000.00 to $60,000.00.

Needless to say, these two factors were serious. I had waited upon God to guide in the choice of property and here were these staggering prices to face, as well as the necessity of locating some miles away from Manila's outskirts.

Then God began to work. An earnest Christian businessman in Manila, hearing of our need, inquired as to the specific property requirements of FEBC. I outlined what was necessary, and he replied that he and his business partner, another Christian man, had a piece of property that might be suitable to our needs. We drove out to the land which is just seven miles from the center of Manila and located on the national highway. The regulations on distance from Manila would have ruled out this property, except that previously licensed prewar local stations were close by. Therefore, the government radio commission accepted this piece of property as valid.

But now the question of the cost of the property remained to be settled. This land consisted of twelve and one half acres valued at approximately $50,000.00 U.S. This amount of property not only would be enough for the station and studios but for housing facilities of station personnel, missionaries assigned to FEBC, and visiting missionaries. An ample portion is already under cultivation and will remain so in order that the station per-

sonnel may have proper amounts of vegetables and
fruits.

After consulting with the two owners of the property
and setting before them the aims of FEBC, we were
offered the entire plot for $20,000.00. The Far East
Broadcasting Company now holds an option to buy the
property for that amount!

John Broger used the last fifty dollars in his pocket to
bind the option. By November 10, the date on which the
option had to be met, $5,000.00 was sent and the land se-
cured. The remaining $15,000.00 had to be paid by Decem-
ber 1!

In the meantime John Broger had returned to the United
States. The need for getting the remaining fifteen thousand
dollars to Manila on time lay heavily on the hearts of Broger,
Bowman and Roberts. Sitting around a table one afternoon,
they talked frankly with each other. If they were going to
worry about this need being met, it wasn't faith. If they
tried to raise the money by one of many methods, it wasn't
God's work. If it was a work of God, He would send it in.
They would not borrow it. It was decided they have a week
of prayer in which time they would commit this problem to
the Lord and let Him work.

The closing day of prayer was November 28—Thanksgiving Day! The day before, they still lacked $4,000.00, but
God had given them the assurance He would meet the
need. That afternoon they sent a cable to the Philippine
committee that $15,000.00 would be sent on time. As they
closed the office that afternoon, with the thought of the
next day being Thanksgiving, there abode in them the peace
and assurance of the promise, "If ye abide in me, and my
words abide in you, ye shall ask what ye will, and it shall be
done unto you."

Friday morning they went to the post office box to get
the mail, but there was none—not a single letter! As they

walked out of the post office, the clerk called from the window and told them they had a package. Upon arriving at the office, they noticed it was not wrapped for mailing, but the lids were crisscrossed to hold the contents in. Ripping the cover off they found more mail than they had ever received in one day and the gifts amounted to $6,062.00!

Of that amount $5,000.00 came from a man living in Chicago, unknown to the men in the FEBC office, but to whose heart the Holy Spirit had spoken as he entered his business office one morning. He said to his secretary, "Send a check for five thousand dollars to those young men out in California who have a vision for building a missionary radio station in the Orient." God had done abundantly above what had been requested!

Dick Rowland, a young man who had completed his training in electronics and who had a vision to serve the Lord in missionary radio, became FEBC's first engineer. Dick was sent to help complete the transmitter being assembled in the midwest.

Because of delays in constructing the transmitter it was decided by the men in the home office they should bring what there was of it to California and finish it in a special "electronics laboratory" made from an old chicken house on the back of Bowman's parents' property. But the trip from the midwest to Los Angeles was not without incident!

A large van-type truck had been given to FEBC, and this was the first trip for it. Because the van body and the cab were not attached, there would be no means of communicating between the two; therefore, a buzzer system was rigged up for signaling. It was decided that one buzz would be "Everything OK," two, "Stop when convenient" and three, "EMERGENCY! STOP!"

Because the ex-army truck had a governor set at a slow 45 miles per hour, the three men became weary of driving across the plains. One at a time would sleep in the van.

Suddenly, the buzzer sounded three times! Then another three times! The driver pulled off the road and the two men ran back to open the door. But when they opened it, they found the Italian boy sound asleep on the floor in between two very heavy pieces of equipment.

"Come on, what goes? This is no time to play!"

"I was sound asleep. What's the idea of waking me up like that?"

"Wake you up," they replied. "Are you kidding? You rang the buzzer, so we stopped."

"What are you talking about? I didn't ring any buzzer. I've been asleep," he said.

At that moment Dick Rowland looked up and saw the heavy load tottering on edge and ready to fall on Julio lying below! He would be crushed! They pulled him out by his heels and quickly adjusted the load so it would be safe. It took all three of them to push it back into place. (And some people don't believe in guardian angels!)

As in any business which takes inventory at the end of the year, the men in the FEBC office carefully noted what God had wrought during their first year:

December 20, 1945—Incorporation of FEBC with $1,000.00, no financial backing, and no permit to build a radio station.

March 25, 1946—John Broger sailed for the Orient to officially contact Far Eastern governments.

June, 1946—Organization of the China Christian Broadcasting System, and subsequent application to the Chinese government for a franchise to erect six stations (still pending).

August, 1946—Organization of the Far East Broadcasting Company (Philippines), Inc.

September 4, 1946—Granting of Philippine franchise to erect two ten-thousand-watt stations (medium and shortwave) in Manila.

October, 1946—Construction of Manila transmitter begun.

October, 1946—Transcription equipment for recording studio in Shanghai purchased and assembled preparatory to shipping.

November 30, 1946—Final payment sent for the twelve and one half acres of property in Manila which would accommodate all radio installations and personnel living quarters.

December, 1946—Passport applications made for first FEBC radio missionary, former Chaplain Arvid Veidmark, of U.S. Army in Philippines, who with his family would soon leave for Manila to begin ground-breaking for transmitter and personnel housing.

A grand total of over fifty-three thousand dollars had been received for the furtherance of this great new endeavor for Christ and His kingdom.

Chapter Three

ON THE AIR

DARK WAR CLOUDS were hanging heavy over China. Generalissimo Chiang Kai-shek's Nationalist government was being driven back by Communist forces from the northwest. In fact, a definite war front could not be established; the Reds had infiltrated the government ranks as well as the military forces and no one could trust the person beside him. Christians were being persecuted; churches that had been built with American money were being confiscated. Surely, China was doomed! The days of the foreign missionary working on China soil were numbered.

In the wise providence of God, men are not always permitted to see too far into the future. Had a franchise been granted to Broger by the National Chinese government, it would have meant that all equipment would have been confiscated by the Communists as they swept across China during those dreadful years. Instead of being an instrument for sending the Good News of peace, from its antennas would have sounded forth lies of the men who had plans for conquering the world.

Unknown to the men of FEBC, the Communists held the scheme of using the ether waves in their master plan of propagating Communist doctrine to the Chinese. Though such a plan has never been revealed to the Free World, it must have been something like this:

1. Set up powerful broadcasting stations to teach Communism to the millions of China.

31

2. Build factories as quickly as possible to produce radio receivers by the thousands.

3. Use both medium and shortwave bands for efficiency.

4. Construct jamming stations in case the capitalists try to broadcast to the Chinese people.

It is a known fact that numbers one and two of the above were accomplished. The only way left to reach China's millions after the last foreign missionary came out was by radio, and the Communists had played right into the hands of Christians!

As missionary leader Peter Deyneka once said, "Nations can build a fence around their land but they can't put a lid on top!" In Christian circles the expression "closed doors" is often used. True, to the foreign missionary, China had become a closed door, but as Paul, writing from prison, said, "Though I be in bonds, THE WORD OF GOD IS NOT BOUND."

Radio waves regard no international boundaries; the highest mountains do not repel them; they are not lost over endless stretches of ocean; both the city dweller amid teeming thousands and the lonely tribesman can be reached the same; to the educated or to the illiterate, radio waves carry the same message.

One is often reminded of the parable of the sower. Some seed fell by the wayside, the Bible tells us. Some fell on rocky ground, some fell among thorns, and some fell on good soil. The Word of God as it is spoken from the lips into the microphone is carried through the components of the transmitter and changed into electrical impulses. From there it is cast forth from the antenna to the heavens and with the speed of light is carried "on wings of the wind."

As in the above parable, some of the Word falls by the wayside—or is assimilated in space. Some is received by those whose hearts are not ready to hear the Truth. Some is picked up by those who seem interested in hearing the message but are carried away with the cares, riches and pleasures of this world. But the promise is that some *will* fall on good ground and bear fruit. Thus the broadcaster, who perhaps never sees his audience face to face, can be encouraged in the fact that God's Word shall not return unto Him void.

The year 1947 held big things for FEBC. Land had to be cleared on the Manila property. The Viedmarks arrived in April with their personal belongings plus a new jeep equipped with a blade for bulldozing and preparing the ground for the building sites.

To the nonprofessional, prices of broadcasting components were staggering; but that wasn't all that was staggering. Over in Manila the Viedmarks were having their problems too. Prices of building materials had skyrocketed since the war. And even if one had a bank full of money, most materials were not available to anybody but the government and contractors on highest priority. The area surrounding the property was infested with Hukbalahap* forces. They made nightly raids, stealing everything they could get their hands on.

Then, to add to all this, there was a deadline to meet. The franchise was good only if they went on the air by 8:00 P.M., April 14, 1948. That meant suitable studios and transmitter buildings had to be constructed out of hard-to-get and very expensive materials. The transmitter had to be completed and checked out before being shipped the seven thousand miles across the Pacific. Missionary personnel would have to arrive to prepare the broadcasts. Thousands of dollars would have to come in before this project could be completed.

Living in a Filipino house already on the property, the Viedmarks worked and supervised the Filipino help. Gravel was not available except by shoveling it out of the creek bed

*Filipino word for Communist forces hereafter referred to as the Huks.

by hand. Although cement was on one of the highest priority lists, not a single day was lost because of not having enough. Through negotiations with the Priority Board, FEBC was placed in the same category as important buildings in Manila. The foundations for the studio and transmitter buildings were poured first, then the floors. Filipinos, working with crude tools, put up the structural parts of the buildings.

A well needed to be drilled, but the cost was estimated at ten dollars a foot, not including the four-inch casing. Finally, an ex-army man, dying of TB and wanting to do something for God which would last after he was gone, offered to do it at a fraction of that cost. And to the surprise of all, perfectly pure water was found in abundance at 750 feet.

And did it ever make a difference to bathe after they had water! Not having procured storage tanks yet, they rigged up a gas engine pump at the well. After a hard day of work, showers were in order, but there was a priority problem! In the dark, one at a time, they would go up to shower under the gushing cold water from the four-inch pipe. The arrangements were: if one heard the engine running at the pump after dark, he should not go near. Someone was taking a shower!

By fall the two main buildings were partially finished. Even though there was correspondence between the office and Manila, it seemed to Viedmark the folks in America had forgotten all about the deadline. Finally, an urgent cablegram was sent to Los Angeles:

> "The Philippine Government demands that FEBC
> go on the air by April 14, 1948!!!"

Already working long hours, the men put the finishing touches on the transmitter and got it crated for shipment. How badly it needed to be thoroughly checked out before sending overseas—but that would have to be put off because of the time element. Passport applications had to be processed for the new recruits leaving for the field. Mr. and Mrs. Broger would be leaving for Manila to expedite the project. Dick Rowland would be helping set up the transmitter after spending months as one of its builders. The capable Dick Handlos, with his family, would be working at Christian Radio City as chief engineer. Mr. Kreps left a manual arts teacher's position and the Gearys felt the Lord was leading them from a mechanical engineering position to help establish this new undertaking in the Philippines. Helen Barker was well qualified for her job in directing the health programs so necessary as a public service, and her musical talents would be put to good use.

One of the times the office staff will never forget was when John Broger went to the phone and called the Pacific Far East Steamship Company and said, "I'd like to reserve space for 18 passengers and 52 cubic tons of equipment on your next boat leaving for Manila."

The voice came back: "Fine. That is 18 passengers at $450.00 a passage, and 52 tons at $40.00 a ton. Altogether that will be $10,180.00. Would you like to send us a check for this amount?"

After a decided pause in the conversation, John finally said, "Would you please reserve that space for us, and the last day you have to have the money or cancel the space, give us a call?"

Every time the phone rang there was a quick rise in pulse, for the bank account stood at $6.00! But on the day the phone did ring and the Steamship Company advised the sailing date, the money was in the bank!

On February 23, 1948, half of the eighteen FEBC staff, plus fifty-two cubic tons of equipment sailed out of San Francisco harbor on the S.S. "Indian Bear," the other half sailed later on the S.S. "China Bear." It was humanly impossible to uncrate, set up and test the transmitter, complete the studio, and set up an antenna system by the deadline.

By the time the new personnel arrived, the total had risen to thirty. The Shorts had been transferred from their work in Borneo to work with FEBC. Every man and woman worked as long as they had the strength. Filipino workmen joined in with the Americans to help get the job done. Even the older children could be credited with doing their share. But the deadline—it couldn't be met!

With building material priced so high, they could not buy enough to finish the buildings already started. During this stage of development, one of the worst typhoons hit Manila and for weeks—one time three weeks straight—rain came in torrents. And when it rains in the Philippines, it often blows. At such times the rain literally is driven horizontally, and since most of the houses had siding but no windows, personal items, such as bedding, books and the like were well soaked. Seven used quonset huts were purchased for $450.00—just a fraction of their value—and rebuilt at Christian Radio City.

John Broger, writing from Manila, said:

> . . . There are many problems, but we know there is victory in Jesus. We gather for prayer at 7:15 A.M. and the Lord has continually reminded us that we are more than conquerors in Christ Jesus! We are few in number and the task is tremendous—greater than we could ever expect to accomplish in the natural—but our heavenly Father will give us strength. We have confidence in Him!
>
> We thank God that everyone is in good health even though we have a 14-hour working day. The quonsets are going up steadily, and the transmitter building is well on the way. The electronic equipment is being installed and already we are beginning to thrill in anticipation of on-the-air-day.

Not only were the transmitter, studio equipment, and electric power supply necessary, but the antenna system could not be slighted. Ninety-foot telephone poles were secured from the U.S. Navy, who were willing to give them away to get them off their lot. But the job of getting the poles down the highway and round the corner onto the road approaching Christian Radio City was no small feat! The shopkeepers at the highway intersection, where the poles had to make the turn, were not so pleased with the deadline-conscious engineers as they saw their petite businesses shoved over in the dust as the ends of the poles swung by!

Lifted into place with the help of a heavy army boom, the poles served to hold the 680 feet of antenna wire in the air. It was far from an ideal antenna but would have to do for the present. The most important thing was to *get on the air before the deadline to show proof of performance!*

The pleas of Broger and several of his engineering henchmen resulted in an extension to the time limit. How thankful they were for the extra seven weeks, but they didn't see how they could finish it even then. Days rolled by into weeks and it was soon nearing the day when they were to be on the air or lose the franchise! Could they make it? Only the Lord could bring it about. Their strength was giving out.

Three days before they were to have all equipment ready and on the air, they expected to have the transmitter compeltely wired and ready to test. But something went wrong with one of the circuits, and it had to be repaired.

At the rate they were going, they couldn't test it—even briefly—before the deadline. The antenna lead-in wire was hung up temporarily with some crisscross poles for support. The console and turntables were wired together, then to the control room—with wires untidily braided and lying on the floor. Wires from the power plant were strung across make-shift poles to the rear of the transmitter. Wives prayed constantly that their husbands would not be electrocuted. Often working in water ankle deep, the men had to work with high-voltage power lines, which combination was a veritable powder keg!

Telephone service in Manila was worse than poor after the war. Broger drove downtown the morning of June 4. The station was to be on the air by 8:00 P.M. that evening, or they might as well pack up and leave. Their chances of proving themselves capable of operating a radio station in the Philippines would have terminated. John asked for a few more days. But the more he tried, the more he was sure it would not be granted. He decided to call Christian Radio City and tell them they had to be ready to go on the air— but the line was dead! With roads as they were and traffic snarls in every other block in the downtown area, he knew he would have to get going and keep moving or he could not make it back in time.

Racing through back streets and barely missing pull-carts in the roads, Broger burned up every piece of road he could between traffic jams. Finally, just before 6:00 P.M. he raced up the road—dust flying—and came to a sliding stop in front of the transmitter building.

"No extra time granted," he yelled to the men. "We've got to get her fired up right now!"

"But we haven't even tested it once," Dick replied.

"We'll test it on the air!" Broger returned, as he ran to the console to grab a bit of programming he had prepared.

"Handlos, will you start the power plant so that we can get the transmitter warmed up—and don't forget to throw the master switch out there!"

"Have you finished drying the windings on those power transformers yet, Dick?" John continued.

"Well, we've done the best we can but I'm not saying they are right. But we don't have time to check it now."

Children who had been playing around the yard in front

of the transmitter building soon realized something was happening inside with all the yelling and bustling around. Some of the older children went to tell their mothers that the radio was going to work! Before long all the families were standing close to the door with a spirit of anticipation and at the same time praying that they could make the grade.

Broger, sorting some papers at the console, called to Handlos to turn on the transmitter and prepare to go on the air. Over on the panel, needles on the numerous dials started to swing to different positions. With a rather modest grin Dick nodded to John. At that moment, John called in all the staff and with heads bowed, they thanked God for His miraculous help and asked Him to undertake for this very first broadcast.

As the entire staff began singing the great hymn, "All Hail the Power of Jesus' Name, Let Angels Prostrate Fall," John gave the nod to Dick to throw the switch and the first of the Far East Broadcasting Company's transmitters hummed with power as it went on the air at 6:00 P.M., June 4, 1948, releasing the words of this majestic hymn to the waiting airways of the Orient.

With tears flowing freely and hearts welling with indescribable joy, the FEBC staff in Manila stood transfixed, American and Filipino together, as the words of this beautiful song rang out clear and strong:

> Let every kindred, every tribe,
> On this terrestrial ball,
> To Him all majesty ascribe,
> And crown Him Lord of all!

With a flick of the finger, the engineer at the controls motioned to Broger that he was on the air.

"Ladies and gentlemen—this is the initial broadcast of KZAS,* the new "Call of the Orient" station, located in Manila, Philippines.

*Shortly after, the designation was changed to DZAS.

"At this hour of 6:00 P.M. on June 4, 1948, the Far East Broadcasting Company lays before you the foundation for that which we believe to be the challenge of this generation —the challenge to do a work for God, the challenge of faith!

"If the peoples of the Orient have need of anything in this day and time, it is faith—faith in yourselves and your ability to rise above the problems of this chaotic age, but more than that, faith in an eternally wise and loving heavenly Father.

"To this end we, of the Far East Broadcasting Company, have dedicated ourselves. We will serve you to the best of our ability with whatever knowledge we may have or whatever wisdom we may g'ean from those of richer experience.

"We, of the Far East Broadcasting Company, pledge ourselves to the highest ideals of culture and dignity. In all phases of broadcasting we shall endeavor to bring to you that which will lend a very real assistance to the threefold nature of man—physical, mental, and spiritual.

"Friends, these are the reasons for the existence of the Far East Broadcasting Company.

"We are here to serve *you!*

"Thank you, and God bless you."

But alas, after just two short hours of broadcasting, the 1,000-watt transmitter kicked off automatically from an overloaded circuit, and they went off the air. But who could care less now? They had given proof of performance and would not be in danger of losing the precious franchise. It was significant to all who had worked so tirelessly that God had allowed the transmitter to work just long enough to prove itself. After all, it had never been checked before and would have to go through further tests amid a limited broadcasting schedule for the next few weeks.

Aerial view of Christian Radio City, Manila, looking toward Manila.

Studio-administration building and 308-foot antenna tower,
Christian Radio City, Manila.

Bowman, Broger and Roberts, founders.

Overseas studios and controls, Christian Radio City, Manila.

Partial view of tape library, Program Department, Christian Radio City, Manila.

Modern "Portable Missionary" radios are located in each of the provinces and on every inhabited island of the Philippines as well as in five additional countries in Asia.

Indian Christians record Gospel programs in New Delhi studio.

50,000-watt RCA overseas transmitter. Chief engineer, Francisco Matias, at controls, Bocaue, Philippines.

Villagers gather around "PM" in headhunter country.

Isabelo Montejo, "PM" Department Director, places a "PM" among Ilongot tribesmen in Nueva Dizcaya, Philippines.

Balik Luna, the mayor of 5,000 friendly but extremely shy Mangyan tribesmen in the mountains on the Island of Mindoro. Balik is one of those who have received Christ as Saviour. This "PM" is one of the several that minister to his people.

"Jesus loves me, this I know." Little Filipinos listen to a "PM" radio.

Chapter Four

FORTY TONS OF STEEL

FOR SEVERAL YEARS a group of young Filipinos had been meeting together for prayer. Their purpose was to ask the Lord in what direction they should release their spiritual energies. In fact, before they banded together as the Filipino Prayer Band, several of them had carried a burden for a vital work in the Philippines.

One of the group, Max Atienza, had seen much action as a guerilla fighter during the war and had testified often to the fact that listening to the radio had kept his spirit high during those rugged days. From America came the promise by shortwave radio that MacArthur would be coming back. Max wondered if the day would ever come when they might see a Christian radio station set up in the Philippines. To this end, the group of young men prayed.

Without knowing anything about the groundwork being laid by the first FEBC personnel on the Islands, the men not only prayed about it but sought to find out what would be necessary to start such a project. As they met to pray one evening, Max excitedly walked into the room and announced, "What do you know, fellows, a Christian group from America by the name of Far East Broadcasting Company has received a permit from our government to set up a radio station here in Manila."

After some discussion as to what they could do to help, the men prayed earnestly for this new project. At the close of the meeting they took up a collection among themselves, and the sum totalled $20.00 (U.S.), which was no small amount for that place and time.

In two places, 7,000 miles apart, God had challenged men
of different nationalities to the practicality of broadcasting
in the Orient. Not long after, Max Atienza joined the FEBC
staff as a preacher and announcer in the Tagalog language.

With such a poor antenna system KZAS's signal was not
covering too great an area. Even some parts of Manila were
not being reached consistently because of physical conditions. And yet, once in a while they would get listening reports from far distances. A captain on a ship 1,500 miles
from Manila wrote that he had heard them and had been
listening for several days. But they needed a new antenna
—and they needed it badly! The station had been such a
drain on the home office they felt they shouldn't ask for
that kind of money right now. Besides, they were building
two shortwave transmitters in Manila—using mostly surplus
parts—to increase their listening audience manyfold.

Driving through the streets of Manila and through the
countryside, several of the men spent days making reports
on the areas they were covering. But reports, accurate or
not, did not satisfy the man at the mike who was wondering
if his message was getting out.

It was a thrill when the first letter arrived in FEBC's
Manila post office box. For many days a barber in downtown
Manila had been listening to the broadcasts from Christian
Radio City. Often the men who had their hair cut would
linger behind and listen. José, one of the regular customers,
was an atheist—a man who made it clear to everyone he
met that he didn't believe there was a God. Not only did he
make his views plain but tried to sell everyone else his bill
of goods.

Haircut day came for José. As Filipino barbers take longer
in cutting than our superspeed American barbers, José was
in the chair for at least a half hour. Added to this, the barber,
who was not a Christian, talked his long-haired friend into

a shave and massage. All this time the radio was blaring away with a program he had never heard before.

The shop normally closed at 8:00 P.M., but that night the men sat motionless until KZAS signed off the air. Leaving without saying a word, the atheist started home. The next night he returned to listen to the broadcast. In fact, he was a regular sitter from that time on.

One night, in the privacy of his own room, José was humbled before the One who had borne his sins. Without anyone speaking to him or helping him, he accepted Christ as his personal Saviour as had been presented on the radio. Not long after, the ex-atheist led his barber friend to the Lord, and several of the other barber shop listeners came to know Christ.

Out on the national highway about six miles from the city of Manila lived a man who had been engaged in a rather unusual "profession." For several years he had done very well in robberies. His wife knew what was going on and dreaded the day when he would be caught and sent to prison. The truth was being held from their small children.

During one of his jobs, he had "appropriated" a nice table model battery radio. It was the first he could call his own! Since his "occupation" called for work after dark, his afternoons were spent in listening to his newly acquired radio.

After listening for several hours, he said to his wife, "You know, that must be a strong station. And I can't figure it out. They don't have any commercials." His wife kept on working without looking up.

"And another thing, the music is so nice," he added.

Still looking down at her work, she muttered, "Sure, the music sounds good, but what about the talk? It makes me feel awful when that man speaks about God, and especially when he talks about sin."

"Well, I haven't said anything to you but I've been thinking about finding where this place is and going to see them," he added.

"You don't have to go far. It's right across the field—over there." Walking over to the open window, she pointed to the unfinished buildings and the ninety-foot antenna poles in the distance.

Hearing there were some foreigners over there, he decided he'd better not go near lest his "profession" be found out. But for days he stayed by the radio listening to every message. Conviction of heart and soul became so strong he had no rest; added, of course, to the constant fear of being caught for one of his robberies, his burden was too crushing to bear. He finally gave up one afternoon. As the Spirit of God dealt with him, he realized he would have to give up his robberies and even pay back his "debts." The day came when he threw himself down before the radio and confessed his sin to Christ. True, there was a struggle. Making restitution for his misdeeds seemed to be one of the things that held him back. But when he faced this squarely and said, "Yes," the struggle was over.

Having done some jewelry repair work prior to his robberies, he decided to set up a small business and try to make a living for his growing family, plus paying back the people from whom he had stolen. It was a steep uphill grade, but with victory in every step through the Lord. He never ceased to give thanks to the Lord for the radio broadcasts that were coming in so strong. After all, the new station was less than a mile away!

The problem of a better antenna plagued the radio missionaries as they realized how much better their signal would be getting out if they could dispense with the telephone pole antenna system.

In the meantime, Bob Bowman exchanged places with John Broger in Manila. The engineers put the pressure on

Bowman for a new tower, but the answer was always, "No money."

Diplomatically, Bowman asked the men what they figured they needed for a new tower. The answer was, "We should have a 300-foot steel tower. One from the States, plus freight out here, would run about $25,000.00." And they didn't bat an eye when they gave that estimate!

One day a man called Christian Radio City on the telephone. He was an executive from one of the big wireless companies. He said, "I hear you are looking for an antenna. We bought three of them from war surplus. They are 300 feet high, self-supported by four legs 60 feet apart at the base, and weigh 80,000 pounds apiece. We paid $3,700.00 each for these towers and it cost us $1,500.00 to ship them over here to Manila. Now we find we need only two. Would you like to have the third one for what we have in it?"

Bob returned, "My, we surely would like to have it. That is exactly what we need. But we don't have that kind of money!"

The pleasant voice on the other end continued. "Well, let's talk it over anyway." Bowman went right to his office to see him.

For two hours the executive asked questions. "How is it financed?" he asked. "Where does the money come from?" He had trouble understanding about faith.

Before the conversation was finished that afternoon he asked what they would be willing to pay. Bowman rather sheepishly said, "We have about three hundred dollars in our account at present. That is only peanuts, of course."

"Let me cable my home office in the States and see what they will let it go for," the gentleman returned.

The next afternoon the same man telephoned Bowman and said, "My company advises that you can have the tower for THREE HUNDRED DOLLARS!"

Within a few days heavy trucks were rolling in from the

highway with forty tons of steel precut and formed for a massive tower that would reach into the sky three hundred and eight feet! The wood crating material holding the pieces together would have cost—in Manila—far more than $300.00!

Byrd Brunemeier and his family arrived in Christian Radio City shortly before the antenna was delivered. Being a radio engineer—plus having natural mechanical abilities—he was qualified for the job of setting up the tower. Don Geary and Byrd were in charge of the entire job. Several Filipino men were hired for helpers, and one professional rigger completed the crew. It took days to get the steel sorted.

One phase of the tower project came as a blow to the staff of Christian Radio City. When the contractor submitted his price for the four concrete footings—two thousand dollars—it meant they would have to put off the construction, because they had no such amount on hand.

One day, petite Mrs. Chua Kian Tiong, who was doing the Chinese programs, walked by the piles of steel. Bob Bowman was standing near where the tower footings were to be poured. "Why isn't the tower being assembled?" Mrs. Chua inquired.

"Only one reason," Bob replied. "We lack $2,000.00 for the foundations."

She shook her head as she turned around to leave. Bob heard her murmur, "Too bad, too bad!"

A week later as Mrs. Chua came to the recording studio, she quietly excused herself for a few minutes and went over to Bowman's office where she laid a white envelope in front of him and departed. When he opened it, he was utterly thrilled beyond words. Before him lay $2,000.00 she had collected from her Chinese Christian friends. By faith (plus a little works) she had removed the last hindrance to the job of erecting the tower.

Week after week the work went on. Every piece of heavy steel angle iron had to be lifted in place by the winch. Men working on the tower were held securely by their safety belts. But at times they had to depend on their hands as they jockeyed around for another position.

Everything was going as usual on the afternoon of May 22, when suddenly there was a screech from the cable and a heavy steel beam swung over on the Filipino rigger. His body went limp! Blood was streaming from his head. Both Don and Byrd shinnied over on the cross-members to see what had happened.

Response to their calls for help brought out men from the studio building. "Get an ambulance quick! Mike is hurt badly!"

Bowman ran to call but the phone was busy! After many attempts, he got through to an ambulance, but they said they didn't want to make the trip because it was too far, and besides, it was across the county line! He called other places and the same excuses were given. Finally, he persuaded one of the hospitals to send its ambulance.

In the meantime the men had made a stretcher and were lowering unconscious Mike down with the use of the winch.

Two hours later the ambulance arrived from downtown Manila about the same time Mike's limp body was lowered to the ground. The next hours were tense. After surgery, the doctors gave him a fifty-fifty chance of recovery. Four days later, as he was showing signs of getting along well, they put him in a room with a fan blowing air directly over him. Two days later he passed away after contracting pneumonia!

Even though this accident was a shock to all, it dared not set them back in the erection of the tower. With safety belts a bit more snug and extra precautions observed at every turn, the tower continued to go skyward until a great day in the second week in June. That was the day when Don and Byrd climbed down from the top and shook hands at the bottom of the 308-foot, 80,000-pound steel tower!

All the time the tower was going up, other FEBC engineers were working feverishly to complete a new 6,000-watt medium wave transmitter to replace the original 1,000-watt equipment.

Chapter Five

DISAPPOINTMENT

A GROUP OF YOUNG PEOPLE in America were challenged with the need of purchasing two large 50,000-watt diesel generators, costing $7,500.00 (war surplus price). The last of April, 1949, the two units arrived in Christian Radio City and were put into service immediately.

Expensive parts for the new 10,000-watt transmitter being built in Manila were draining the kitty in Los Angeles. As the engineers knew all too well, there was still inadequate power for the present transmitters plus those soon to go on the air, for they already foresaw the need for two more 2,000-watt shortwave transmitters on the Overseas Service.

Bob Bowman was looking around for a 30,000-watt generator but found the price to be $18,000.00. He stopped looking! Happening by a large international broadcasting station one day, he began talking to the diesel engineer, and was asked, "How are you getting along? How are the new generators working out for you?"

"Fine, but we are looking for another 30,000-watt job. We'll soon have the big ones overloaded," Bob replied.

"Is that so?" he asked. (Bob didn't tell him they didn't have the money to buy one—just said they were looking around for one!)

Then the engineer added, "Wonder if we could help you out." And that was all he said.

Several weeks later Bowman stopped in again as he was going by. The engineer approached him and said, "Say, about that generator you need, see this one over here? It's

a 30,000-watt generator that we just overhauled. How
would you like to have it?"

"What do you mean, 'like to have it?' "

"Just take it."

"You're kidding!"

"No, I'm not. It's yours."

Not long after, they put the generator on their trailer
and hauled it down to Christian Radio City in Manila. Again,
God had met the need in a miraculous way.

*   *   *   *

Letters were beginning to come in to Christian Radio
City. Not only were they an encouragement to the staff
but they were used to put impetus on the job of completing
the new transmitters. One letter said:

> DEAR FRIENDS:
>
> I've always listened to dance music on my radio, but
> last night I happened to turn the dial to your station and
> was surprised to hear my own language on the air. I
> live a long way from Manila and this is the first time
> we have heard DZAS.* I am sorry my language is only
> on twice a week. We do not have any missionary here.
> We do not have a pastor. I have never met any Chris-
> tians. The thing you are talking about thrills my heart.
> I became convicted by the heaviness of sin in my heart.
> Last night, when I heard of the Lord Jesus Christ, I
> wanted Him to help me. Now I feel so happy. Please
> tell me what has happened to me!
>
> > Sincerely,
> > H. GARCIA

Another man wrote:

> My whole family has been listening to your broadcast

*By order of the Philippine Radio Control Board the call letters of all
Philippine broadcasting stations had been revised. The FEBC station from
that time on has been designated as DZAS.

for a year now, and at last we are convinced that Jesus Christ is the Son of God, the true God, and that your religion is correct. We have all accepted Him as our personal Saviour.

Without fanfare, late one afternoon the first shortwave transmitter of 1,000 watts went on the air. The only dedication service held was by the three engineers who stood in front of the panel and bowed for prayer as the tubes were warming up prior to going on the air.

More studio space was urgently needed to handle the extra programming. By this time the tape library was no small department. Three walls in one room—and not a small one—were covered with shelves and lined with boxes of plastic magnetic recording tape, well catalogued and ready for immediate use by any of the staff doing programming. Wives and older girls of the staff graciously accepted the jobs of caring for the libraries. Another wing was built on the studio building to accommodate studio B and offices.

Gilberta Walton, FEBC's first lady engineer and one possessed with a wealth of broadcasting background, arrived in Christian Radio City to take over the directorship of all programming.

As the Far East Broadcasting Company's work became more popular with Christians in America, missionaries, mission leaders and world travelers were sure to include Manila and the side trip to Christian Radio City on their itinerary.

The multiplicity of programs in so many different languages was a nightmare at times to the still fairly new radio missionaries. Limited Gospel programming was being broadcast to China, Russia, Viet Nam, Thailand, Indonesia, and, of course, to the extreme limits of the Philippines.

One of the guests at Christian Radio City was David Morken, who was Youth for Christ director of Shanghai, China. After his return to China, he wrote the FEBC staff a most encouraging letter:

DEAR BROTHERS AND SISTERS IN CHRIST:

I wish I had words adequate to tell you how I feel
about the work of Far East Broadcasting Company. As
I listen to the well-planned professionally produced
Christian programs coming from Christian Radio City,
Manila, I am reminded of the Apostle John's statement
of purpose for writing his Gospel: "These are written,
that ye might believe that Jesus is the Christ, the Son
of God; and that believing ye might have life through
His name." Even as John had carefully selected the
testimonies of competent witnesses in order that we may
have life by believing that Jesus is the Christ, the Son of
God, so station DZAS is planning each program that
men throughout the Far East might have life.

It was indeed one of my great joys to be your guest
and see what great things the Lord is doing. It was
wonderful to learn how God had been preparing men
for this tremendous task since their childhood, yes,
even before they were Christians. And how, after much
training and preparation, He put the urge down in their
hearts to do what He had planned—an urge that would
drive them through and over every obstacle; an urge
that cries, "There is only one program of importance: the
bringing of the Good News of salvation to all men"; an
urge that cries, "I am ready not to be bound only, but
also to die for the name of the Lord Jesus."

We thank God for the entire FEBC staff. In the words
of Habakkuk, "Stand stark still. Stare. A work is being
wrought in your days. Ye will not believe when it is
recounted."

With much love and appreciation,

I am,

Yours in Christ,
DAVID MORKEN

*   *   *   *

About one year after DZAS went on the air, a letter which indeed bore sad news arrived in Christian Radio City. The Philippine government was young and struggling. Due to certain technicalities the Radio Control Board did not renew the license on DZAS!* This in no way affected the license on the shortwave transmitters, but to realize the voice being sent out over the Philippines would be hushed was more than the radio missionaries could understand. Humbling periods of prayer followed for days. They contacted certain men who had influence in the government, but to no avail.

As the staff met for prayer one morning, the Lord led Bob Bowman to read a passage of Scripture which seemed to speak to everyone in the room: "Other sheep I have which are not of this fold."

It was a short sentence, but oh, so striking! FEBC dared not confine its efforts of getting the Gospel out to only the Philippines and other countries close by. To the north lay the Japanese Islands with ninety million souls. To the south—hundreds of islands, large and small, with millions of Indonesians, tribesmen, Chinese and Indians—so many without the Gospel. To the west lay the lands of Southeast Asia divided into Viet Nam, Laos, Cambodia, Malaya, Thailand and Burma. Millions speaking a diversity of languages—multitudes without Christ!

Then, to the northwest was the massive land of China. At this very time, missionaries were fleeing from Communist-controlled areas. Literally hundreds of thousands of Chinese were starving to death. In their ruthless attempt to conquer China, nothing stopped the aggressors as they swept through villages and towns, promising a better way of life "for the future," but wounding and killing innocent Chinese every

*It should be noted here that all radio broadcasting stations are licensed on a yearly basis. Only when proof of providing a service is established with the Radio Control Board can the license be extended for another year. This is true in most countries. However, a long-term franchise for continued operation has been granted FEBC by the Philippine Congress.

foot of the way. Across the countryside and massed in the cities were 700 million souls—many of whom knew not Christ, the Son of God, nor had they even heard of Him. They must not forget Russia, the very seat of godless Communism. Millions also, behind the iron curtain, were not permitted to hear the Truth.

Could it be the Lord was forcing FEBC to consider more the possibilities of shortwave radio and concentrate on propagating the Good News of salvation to the whole of Asia? As heads were bowed in prayer that morning, hearts were burdened as they thought of the souls for whom Christ died, yet without knowledge of Him.

What has been the course of Communism? Let's let history tell the stark truth:

The massacre in 1918 of the entire Russian royal family and their servants in a cellar in Sverdlovsk; mass terrorism against the kulaks and priests; the famine of 1921-23 with 22 million starving; the mass shooting and exile of six million peasants in 1929-32; the famine of 1933 with between five and ten million dying of starvation; the mock trials and executions or deportations to Siberian concentration camps of ten million during 1928-38, the trials and purges of government officials of 1928-38; the debauchery and rapings of the peoples in western Russia by the Red Army in 1943-45 —this is only a partial list!

Let's look at what happened in eastern Europe:

In a few minutes hundreds of men and women were lying dead or wounded on the ground while others crouched for cover behind statuary and columns, or lay flat on the pavement. A column of rioters marched with arms outstretched into machine-gun fire. Students were killed en masse by Soviet tanks. The country's railroads, factories and mines were at a standstill; the city of Budapest was without light, heat, transportation, communications, or food, with thousands of unburied dead lying in its rubble-filled streets, and fires burning in hundreds of buildings.

Pastor Peter Chu Pong, from Asia, testifies:

> The Communists held an accusation meeting to accuse me, my wife, and the elders and deacons in our church of being imperialists. They tied our hands with long rope and forced us to kneel on the platform of our church assembly hall with signs around our necks which said, "Guilty Crime." They slapped our faces, kicked our bodies, and poured cold water on our heads. They made my children stand and watch. If they cried, the Communists beat them. They wanted me to confess that I was an imperialist agent. They wanted me to reject Christ, give up my church, and admit that the only god was Mao Tse Tung . . .

We often think of Communism as a big political machine. It is more than that. Communism is a religion—a godless religion. It is anti-Christian. And yet, its ardent followers use the very methods the early church employed and which we still use today as means of evangelism. Student movements, youth rallies, conferences, groups, or "cells" organized to promote their cause locally, the use of attractive printed material provided reasonably, propaganda spread round the world by radio are but a few ways this diabolical movement spreads its pernicious doctrines. God and His Son, Jesus Christ, are excluded and not only left out, but those who wish to follow their Master are persecuted even unto death.

From the Kremlin and Peking come lies, yet flowered with appealing ideas and dogmas. In forty short years Communism has swept in its grip one third of the world's population, not by love—but by bloodshed; not by truth—but by lies! The fight against Communism is a spiritual warfare—for the souls of men are at stake!

FEBC engineers were determined to press the unfinished

shortwave transmitters through to completion as soon as possible, while the rest of the staff started working with all their energy to produce programs in the languages of these other countries. They had fine cooperation from missionaries of many denominational and independent missions. Letters were sent out to encourage more national workers to tape programs on their fields.

Chapter Six

PORTABLE MISSIONARIES

As UNEXPECTEDLY as the first letter had come from the Radio Control Board, just two months later the second arrived. During those two months nothing could seemingly be done to correct the situation. Unceasing'y, the staff prayed that God would somehow undertake. No particular ray of hope developed as they ripped open the envelope. The contents appeared to be more or less a form letter, but scanning through the second parag:aph, it was evident the letter contained good news.

While not exactly apologizing for the interruption of DZAS's schedule—but almost—the Radio Control Board was pleased to advise that DZAS was licensed to return to the air immediately! Staff members praised the Lord for His definite answer to prayer.

Within minutes after the license was received, DZAS was back in service broadcasting the Gospel to the Philippines.

* * * *

Generally speaking, the Filipinos would be considered poor people according to American standards. As is seen in so many countries of the world, excluding America and parts of Europe, there are two classes of people: the very rich and the very poor—there is no middle class. Because of better farming conditions in the Philippines, the poor class have a higher standard than in countries like India and China. Though many of the families do not have luxury items, most of them at least have food on their tables, clothes on their backs, and a place to sleep.

The Filipino farmer has to work hard and long hours

for the food he provides for his family. Any surplus can be sold, but the profit is low, and there are so many essential things to buy. The more prosperous farmer may own a worn-out jalopy which saps his pocketbook for repairs, but it gives him prestige. A more sensible farmer will proudly own more water buffalo than he really needs, and then can rent or loan his extra beasts.

Rural Filipino houses are of simple construction. Erected on stilts six to eight feet off the ground, the house is made of rough mahogany lumber with woven bamboo or rattan mats used for walls, and thick grass or cane matted together for a roof. The floor is usually made from home-planed mahogany boards. Windows are open but have a bamboo mat which can be placed over the opening in case of rain and wind. Furniture is on the crude side and pictures of all description adorn the otherwise bare walls. Most urban areas are not blessed with electric power; therefore, kerosene lamps and lanterns are used. Only a few rural homes are able to own a battery-powered radio.

Numerous mission groups have missionaries stationed in scattered places in the Philippines. It is hard to believe there are over 7,083 islands in the Philippine archipelago and only 400 are inhabited. The land area is 115,000 square miles with a population of 28 million. The Filipinos are considered to be of Malayan extraction. There are also a small percent of Chinese and Indonesians living on the islands. To reach all these people with the Gospel would take literally thousands of missionaries and hundreds of thousands of dollars.

As DZAS returned to service after its brief rest, the staff was challenged with the need of reaching more people; but there was one big hindrance—so few radios outside Manila. Two possibilities came to mind: they could encourage people to buy small battery-powered receivers, or they could provide some on a loan basis.

Running into a snag on the first plan, they found very few could afford to own a receiver of their own. The only thing to do was to build well-designed and constructed receivers and put them in villages where no one owned a radio. As the plan was being developed, someone came up with the idea they were "portable missionaries," and that was the very name given them from that time on.

The design of the first PM's, as they were soon nicknamed, underwent numerous changes until a satisfactory circuit proved successful under rigid tests. Due to fungus growth because of high humidity, every part of the set had to receive special treatment. A workshop was set up in one of the buildings where assembly-line methods of construction speeded up the output. Homer Kreps was kept busy building the cabinets out of durable Philippine wood. Because of lack of electricity in most areas, the sets were powered with a heavy-duty battery which would last about six months under normal service. Each PM cost about thirty dollars.

Several reasons were behind the decision to pretune the PM's. Because of the limited life of the batteries, their high cost, and even the weight factor in packing them far upcountry, FEBC staff thought it best to keep the use strictly for their programming. And besides, far too much Communist propaganda was being broadcast to Asian countries. Most certainly FEBC didn't want to provide such a convenience to the Reds! The PM's were put in different barrios* for use by all the people but in the care of one responsible person. Reports had to be filled out each month as to how many villagers listened to the programs.

Someone gave a good description of a PORTABLE MISSIONARY:

1. Preaches the Word of Life many hours daily without tiring.

*Philipino word used for village.

2. Speaks any language or dialect.
3. Gives the best in Gospel music.
4. Needs no allowance!
5. Eats no rice!
6. Will not contract tropical disease.
7. Can be carried to the most remote village by missionaries or native workers and left there to continue to minister when the missionary finds it necessary to travel on. It may be carried by responsible natives into regions inaccessible or hostile to missionaries.

Almost simultaneously with the development and distribution of the PM's, the letters from listeners started to pour into Christian Radio City. A few unedited portions are given:

From Pacita T. Pacheco, Nueva Ecija:

Our hearts overflow with satisfaction whenever we hear your preaching to sinners, for it draws so many of us who forget God to believe in Him. We always tune in your program at 8:00 P.M. and listen to your preaching. Not only we, but also our neighbors are blest, even those with darkened minds and filthy hearts begin to remember Him who hung on the Cross for the sins of mankind.

From S. M. Sison, Pangasinan:

I was really touched by those wonderful messages you have delivered over the radio, and I think it is my prime duty to accept them. I long to become a Christian and I long to serve God in the remaining days of my life.

From Ricardo De La Cruz Paco, Manila:

Truly, sir, my heart is too full of unexplainable emotions that I am utterly wanting for the proper words to use but to no avail. I cannot exactly describe the kind

of emotion that pervades within me that sometimes I
feel I would just about burst with it! It is elation, joy,
surging happiness, faith, understanding and above all,
love that turns everything and gives everything a rosy
hue. Ever since I heard your broadcast, as I go about
every day hunting work, I am brimming with happiness.
I have never been so understanding, or forgiving, never
so full of faith. Now I know that to be a believer and to
be loving for the teachings of the Lord Himself is to be
a Christian.

And from Rev. W. Denton, missionary in Panay:

Just before leaving Canton, China—ahead of the Com-
munist armies—we were in the home of a Christian
Chinese. How happy we were to hear the message in
Cantonese when we tuned in on DZH6.

Permission to place a PM in Bilidib prison was granted by
the warden. He also requested a schedule of programs so
he could choose those which he would like the prisoners to
hear. These Gospel programs were relayed over the prison's
public address system to the 6,000 prisoners within its his-
toric walls.

In a letter from Christian Radio City to America, Bob
Bowman wrote:

Praise God for six hours of daily broadcasting on
DZAS, DZH6 and DZH7. (The last two are shortwave
stations for the Philippine Service.) The seed of the
Word is being sown. Evidences show that God is doing
a work in many hearts.

Where the Spirit of God is moving there are also
trials. Night before last a tube in the 5,000-watt transmitter blew out. We didn't have a spare tube on hand
but God supplied through a loan of one from another
station. This tube must be replaced and a spare purchased in case a similar emergency arises in the future.
The two will cost a total of $800.00. Pray the Lord shall

enable us to purchase them so the Gospel will not be
hindered for a single hour.

* * * *

An electrical storm was forming upcountry from Christian
Radio City. With high steel towers, thousands of feet of
copper wire strung in the air, and radio equipment by the
ton, engineers are always a bit more on their toes when
lightning comes close.

Downpours of rain sent everyone scurrying to close their
windows. Along with sheets of rain, streaks of lightning
were striking nearer each minute. A bolt from the sky
pierced down through the antenna array of one of the shortwave transmitters. With a thud, one end of the wire hit the
ground. At that moment Max was preaching in the Tagalog
language in studio C.

After waiting for a few minutes, Bob Bowman thought
he would make a dash home since he had been up long
hours that day. But just as he got outside, he saw the form
of a man climbing up the 308-foot tower. Bowman ran
over to call him to come down. It wasn't necessary to
fix it during the storm. But as Bob got closer, he decided
he better not shout since it might scare Byrd and he would
lose his footing. The rain had ceased temporarily but the
tower was slippery. Brunemeier was clad in only a shirt
with the sleeves removed, slacks, and tennis shoes—his usual
working attire.

Bob patiently waited and watched Byrd fasten the antenna back to the top of the tower and start to come down.
Jumping from the last steps, Byrd whirled around to make
a dash for the transmitter building, but paused as he saw a
man standing there. Bob thought he should be gently re-
proved for risking his life to repair the antenna in such a
storm but was unable to get anything out.

With deliberateness, Byrd turned to Bowman and said,

"But Bob, for every minute that antenna was down, someone was not hearing the Gospel."

He ran back to the transmitter building while Bob continued on to his house. Sleep was difficult for awhile as Bob thought of the dedication of the staff. Praise to God welled up within him as he gave thanks for the men and women who would not only risk their lives but work endless hours, day and night, to send the precious Word out in every direction.

* * * *

A letter of appreciation was sent to FEBC for the PM placed in the home of Mrs. Mercedes Benitz Sable who wrote (unedited):

> We thank Him who is loving and kind to His people in supplying all the things needed in this world. He gave us this wonderful radio which is a very good instrument in bringing many people to come closer and closer to Jesus.
>
> Since this portable radio was loaned to us, many of the inhabitants of this place and neighboring barrios came to see this radio, the fact that they heard the news which said, "Mr. Sable has a wonderful box that sings and talks!" This was the talk of the barrio people before. We know pretty well that people living in the rural places like our place seldom hear the radio, as most of the people have not yet seen the radio. They hear the word "radio" but they have not seen what the real radio looks like. Some were very ignorant about it.
>
> One day we were surprised to see many people coming at home. We thought they were going to town to shop so that they just dropped in at home for some important matters. When we asked what the matter was, they answered that they came purposely for the radio. "Well," I said, "would you care to hear the Lord speak?" They smiled a great desire.*

*It is worthy to ponder this expression, "They *smiled* a great desire."

At the first sound from the radio, everybody stood and
tried to peep and peep. They were surprised. They
thought it was only the box that was talking, but because we could see them very eager to know about it,
we explained how the box speaks and sings.°°

At about five o'clock in the afternoon, many came
again. They asked so many questions. The small children came also marching one by one until at last there
was no more room in the house. After the Ilocano°°°
program was over, they said, "Some more Ilocano; we
want to hear what we can understand!" But we could
do nothing; there was not more Ilocano program that
followed.

Every afternoon although the rains would come, they
came, carrying with them their shades and hats. They
would come hurrying as if they were very, very hungry
for food they had not eaten for a long time.

Last month thieves entered into our house. They
were three that came inside the house and one was
their guard outside. They had pistols. Before they entered the house we were very happy. We didn't think
that such a thing would happen to us. I was singing the
Ilocano hymn "Yield Not to Temptation." I had not
finished singing the first stanza when the thieves entered. I could not recognize them because they wore
big hats. "Oh!" with a surprise, I shouted unconsciously.
The first man that entered the house said, "Don't move!
Don't talk! If you shout, I'll kill you with this pistol!"
We all surrendered!

While we were held at gunpoint, the other thieves
looked in our trunk, boxes, and one of them saw the
radio on the cupboard. Wondering if it worked, he
turned it on and the first thing we heard was Max
Atienza preaching in Tagalog! These men understood
Tagalog and listened to the whole sermon from one end
to the other! As soon as it was finished, they turned off

°°A radio engineer would have been interested in that explanation!
°°°Another language in the Philippines.

the radio, and politely bowed to us and backed out the door!

Really, it's hard to believe this story but because God is very kind to us, all things are possible. Without this radio, perhaps we would be physically maltreated, because we heard later what they did to all the people in the rest of the houses they went to.

My radio is a comfort and help. I know God has given it to me. I'll use it to help to save others. If we lose our wonderful radio, I would feel as if we lost a member of the family. We hope for more blessings and hope to pray for His care and guidance to us day by day.

Mrs. Sable was the only Christian in the barrio when the PM was placed in her care. Five years later Mr. Montejo made a PM missionary journey through that part of the country and stopped to visit the Sables. The men of the barrio were busy gathering material for a new church building. Forty families had come to Christ!

Chapter Seven

BOOSTER SHOT

"And ye shall know the truth, and the truth shall make you free."—JOHN 8:32

"If the Son therefore shall make you free, ye shall be free indeed."—JOHN 8:36

FREEDOM BY TRUTH FOR ASIA was the theme of the first Asiatic Seminar of the Far East Broadcasting Company held at Christian Radio City in the fall of 1951.

The purpose of this gathering was to emphasize the necessity for presenting Christ, the truth, as the only means of freedom for Asia and to determine the most effective way of presenting this truth.

Probably one of the biggest boosts to missionary radio, especially for the Orient and other parts of Asia, was when missionary and national delegates from Burma, Hong Kong, Viet Nam, Indonesia, Japan, Malaya, Russia, Thailand and the Philippines assembled to discuss the problems and review the challenge of the task.

John Broger opened the Seminar by saying:

"Today, as never before, the free world in general and Christians in particular face the problem which challenges all the depth of understanding, intelligence and wisdom that can be brought to bear.

"Men and women the world over are becoming increasingly sensitive to the fact that there is a tremendous warfare in the making, a warfare which does not find its solution in any phase of the material realm, whether military,

financial or economic. Something else, so far as the world
sees it, some unknown factor yet unfathomed, must come to
the fore.

> For we wrestle not against flesh and blood, but against
> principalities, against powers, against the rulers of the
> darkness of this world, against spiritual wickedness in
> high places (Eph. 6:12).

"The Apostle Paul had a clear recognition of the fact that
the warfare of his day (which is equally true of the warfare
of today) had tremendous spiritual significance. We oft-
times are able to comprehend the truth of God's Word without being able to fit the reality of that truth into our present-
day situations.

"No doubt it has occurred to most of us that Communism
is not only a political party, not only a concept of life or a
theory of economy. Far more than that, it is akin to extreme
religious fanaticism, for how else could Communism gain
in its converts such tenacity of purpose and such complete
mastery over every realm of mental, political, moral, economic and spiritual life? To fathom these depths of Communism manifests that this battle must be waged in each
and every one of these realms, for it is not possible to stage
a successful warfare of this nature wholly on the basis of
military manpower or production potential, gun for gun,
ship for ship, propaganda for propaganda. For indeed we do
fight this battle against the 'rulers of darkness,' and only on
the basis of godly righteousness and godly precepts and
principles will we be able to understand the nature of this
great warfare.

"Many words have been written and spoken concerning
the natural reasons why Communism must be stopped. Economic and military plans have been made, but it remains
imperative that every plan must find its source of strength
and inspiration in godly righteousness.

"It is not strange that in almost every instance of major wars in the twentieth century one side has represented belief and faith in God, while the opposing side invariably scoffs at a righteous God, and illustrates in almost every phase of its conduct a mockery and derision of every sincere thought or noble action. The leaders of those opposing forces have consistently followed a course evil in design and treacherous in action.

"How necessary then it is that our ideals of what is right be clear-cut and that we be willing to sacrifice any personal desire or interest to the cause of godly truth and right. In the final analysis it makes no difference whether we call it right, truth, conscience, or what you will. The right word, and it must be remembered so, is *righteousness*.

> And before him shall be gathered all nations; and he shall separate them one from another, as a shepherd divideth his sheep from the goats.
>
> And he shall set the sheep on his right hand, but the goats on the left (Matt. 25:32, 33).

"We long today for some plan, some standard by which we may weigh the national conscience of each nation. Of course God will judge individuals, but seemingly the great majority of people in any nation are being driven strongly to a conclusion and a choice between godliness and ungodliness. How is it possible then to set up a principle of judgment? Perhaps this will work. God has allowed a nation to come into existence whose representative government is committed to total violation of conscience. Every action illustrates the spirit of anti-God and anti-Christ.

"This represents an extreme which we will call 'black.' The opposite extreme, which is godly desire and righteousness, we will call 'white.' Nations may find themselves between these two extremes in some shade of 'gray.' The deepness or the lightness of that shade will perhaps depend on

how that nation has followed or rejected its conscience over
the past years in its attitude to the people of that nation,
and of that nation to other nations and people of the world.
If there have been severe violations of this national conscience, there will be less reaction to Communism, and until
each nation makes its decision, once and for all, to follow
the godly precepts of righteous thought and action, there
will continue to be blindness toward ungodly Communism.

"Christians today, in every walk of life, should be the first
to sense the issues at stake in this warfare, for it has to do
not only with results in this life, but far greater, it has tremendous bearing on the eternal relationship with a just and
righteous God. If Christians are not able to fathom the
secrets of this warfare, if Christians are not able, by the
Spirit of God, to understand the full significance of this
battle, who else will be able to point to Him who is the
Way, the Truth and the Life?

"Mobilize in a crusade for Christ. Begin by utter commitment of yourself in prayer and obedience to His Word
and His Spirit. Then, in utter uncompromising teamwork,
let us go forward in the fight for right, discipling all nations, teaching them to observe all which Christ has told
us, constantly remembering that He said, 'Lo, I am with
you alway.'"

Day after day the seminar went on record as having accomplished its goal in the hearts of men from different races.
Open forums were held in the mornings and reports from
various fields given in the afternoons. The evenings were
given over to devotional meetings.

One thing all the delegates wanted to know was: what
about the different transmitters?

On a special tour one of the engineers explained:

"This is the 5,000-watt DZAS transmitter. It is for local
listeners only, and is a part of the Philippine Service. It
covers the Manila area, and is received on the standard

home-style broadcast receivers. The signals from this transmitter are radiated from the tall 308-foot steel tower behind the transmitter building. Although DZAS is only intended for the Manila city area, it reaches out perhaps seventy miles with fairly consistent day-and-night coverage into the provinces. During the night hours it reaches farther out into provincial areas, but with irregular reception conditions.

"Now, over here is the 2,000-watt tropical broadcast band transmitter DZB2 which is primarily intended to serve the listeners of our little PM radios throughout the Philippines. It, of course, is part of the Philippine Service and because of its higher frequency is able to cover most of Luzon during daylight hours, and all the Philippines after local sunset. This transmitter is connected to a beam that concentrates the signal into the Philippines and effectively increases the signal power to 5,000 watts throughout the archipelago. During late night hours DZB2 reaches far outside of the Philippines, particularly during winter months.

"This is our 2,000-watt DZH6 transmitter—third in the group for the Philippine Service. Because of its shortwave frequency, it can be heard fairly well throughout the Philippines either by day or by night. After local sunset, the signals reach out to greater distances and are heard with good strength in China and Japan. DZH6 also uses a directional beam antenna, which points the signal due north and south.* In the center of this narrow radio beam the signal power is effectively increased to 8,000 watts.

"Please step over here and I'll show you DZH7 which is one of our 3,000-watt transmitters in the Overseas Service.

*There is a complexity of shortwave antennas, but most of them are used in the same way as a hunter uses a shotgun. At will, some of them can be pointed in the direction where the signal is to be broadcast; thus, the expressions "beamed" and "target area" are often used in connection with putting shortwave signals right where you want them. The difference between the power of the transmitter and the increase in effective radiated power is due to the fact that the power of the transmitter can be concentrated to cover one area.

During daylight hours it can be heard throughout the Philippines and the closely surrounding overseas countries. During night hours it has greater strength overseas: it is perhaps our best transmitter for general Oriental nighttime coverage. The DZH7 transmitter has two directional antennas. The northeast beam increases this power to 8,900 watts and focuses the signals along an axis northeast by southwest. This is used for listeners in Japan, eastern Russia, the China coast, Indonesia, and Malaya. The other beam antenna is directed east and west, and it increases the transmitter output to an effective 13,500 watts. The signals from this antenna are intended for listeners in Indonesia, Viet Nam, Thailand, Burma, India, Arabia, and East Africa.

"DZH8 works together with DZH7 to comprise the Overseas Service of FEBC. There are certain periods each day when all five 'Call of the Orient' stations transmit the same English programs simultaneously. At other times they are split up into the two groups, at which times local dialects are carried on the Philippine Service, and foreign languages on DZH7 and DZH8. DZH8 is heard best in the Orient during daylight hours. When darkness comes, the signals begin to skip over the immediately surrounding countries and come down in countries farther away. We have received letters from listeners on DZH8 from every continent of the world.

"The DZH8 transmitter is connected to a rather interesting antenna. This is plainly visible above the transmitter building, being some 80 feet tall. The antenna itself is composed of three parallel rods mounted on a boom which is rotatable. This antenna device concentrates the signal into a beam that goes in one direction only, like a searchlight, and as the antenna is turned this beam can be pointed to any desired country. In the center of this beam the 2,000-watt transmitter output is effectively increased to 16,000 watts."

Chapter Eight

FOLLOW-UP

IT IS ONE THING to speak into a microphone, another thing to keep the transmitter working properly; but there is still another very important phase in missionary radio—and that is to keep in touch with the listeners. Many who hear the Gospel are hearing it for the first time. Others are just babes in Christ. Few are mature Christians. Those who are young in the faith usually are clamoring for more light.

Prior to the outbreak of war in the Pacific in 1941, a small group of Manila missionaries conducted a weekly Gospel broadcast over one of the local Manila commercial stations, which was operated by a prewar company (not Christian) known as the Far East Broadcasting Company. What a coincidence! The Gospel broadcast as well as the Filipino-owned station were brought to an abrupt halt by the Japanese invasion and occupation. Later, these missionaries were interned by the Japanese. After a miraculous deliverance in early 1945, these workers were repatriated to the United States.

In 1949, Mr. and Mrs. Cyril Brooks returned to Manila with thoughts turned to the possibilities of a Bible correspondence school. Friends had been speaking to them of the fine work of FEBC. Pleasant memories of Max Atienza flashed through their minds: he had been a student of Mr. Brooks in a Bible school in Manila.

Early in 1950, word came to Mr. Brooks of a new Bible course prepared by Emmaus Bible School. This course was intended to be a means of reaching men for Christ by presenting the truths of the Gospel in a home study course.

After talking to Robert Bowman, who was in Christian Radio City at the time, they decided the two methods could be combined—a radio program of Bible study and a correspondence school, for this is what the FEBC staff had been praying about for some time. As a result, "The Bible School of the Air" was born and correspondence courses were offered free over the air.

A few months later a Tagalog translation was completed and offered in connection with Max Atienza's program, *"Bukas Na Aklat"* (Open Book). It was arranged that Max would handle Tagalog correspondence and questions, but the lessons would be mimeographed and sent out by the staff of the Bible School of the Air.

A missionary friend remarked to Mr. Brooks one time, "You know, this might develop into a full-time job." How true! In two short years 11,459 English courses and 1,840 Tagalog courses had been requested. The Portable Missionary ministry and the Bible School of the Air were started about the same time. No two ministries could have dovetailed more closely.

Ranging from government officials to ordinary villagers, students taking these courses come from nearly every walk of life. The lessons in Tagalog deal mainly with man and his need of God. Written examinations at the end of each of the twelve lessons gauge the aptitude of the students. Follow-up letters are sent out, together with the corrected and graded examination papers. As a result, definite conversions for Christ are garnered.

Within a short time after the start of the Bible Study Broadcasts they sent nearly 800 New Testaments and Bibles in Tagalog, English, and Ilocano to individuals who had written in their requests. Several thousand Gospel tracts were enclosed with these portions.

• • • •

Isabelo Montejo, a little man with a big vision, joined the
FEBC staff in Manila. His job—to be nursemaid to hundreds
of PM's!

There was no letup after the PM ministry got underway.
Requests came in from all over the Philippines. There just
wasn't enough money to build as many receivers as were
wanted. Montejo, or the modern Apostle Paul, as the Manila
staff called him, used to start out with nothing but PM's.
He carried neither purse nor scrip; extra clothes or shoes he
didn't bother with. By living with the people as he went
from barrio to barrio, Montejo made better contact with the
Filipinos. He would travel by bus or rickety truck as far as
the vehicle would go, then start walking until someone
picked him up and carried him farther down the road. Many
times he ended up riding a water buffalo or walking down a
dusty road—or during the rainy season, slipping and sliding
on the muddy trails.

A hard life was nothing new to Montejo. He had followed
the circus as a fire-eater. When the Lord got hold of his
heart, He gained control of a whole life, for Montejo wanted
to serve the Lord the rest of his days.

Not only was there much work out in the field; he also had
to check the monthly reports. When, through neg'ect, a report or two would be slow in coming in, Montejo was quick
to find what was wrong. Sometimes it was a dead battery,
so the person in charge didn't think it was necessary to report. Keeping the PM's operating and new ones distributed
was a man-size job and Montejo was just the man!

A necessary sideline developed in Christian Radio City
as a result of the PM minstry. The PM Clubs are also literature posts. Each month thousands of tracts are placed in
PM Club captains' hands for distribution. Gospel portions
and New Testaments by the thousands are printed for the
Bible Society.

Bud Jillson, in charge of the printing department, keeps an efficient Filipino staff busy on two printing presses around the clock.

Chapter Nine

JAMMING

WITH DETERMINED EFFORTS the Communists were using every means available to gain the rest of Asia. But something was happening! They were not taking the rest of the southeast Asian countries, the Philippines, and Japan as quickly as they had overrun China. Stiff resistance was felt in some places from groups of people who were learning what was taking place in China. Gospel broadcasts beamed to these countries were helping to deter the advance of the Reds.

The Gospel had been beamed to Russia for many months. It was the only country from which Christian Radio City had not received a listener response. Yet, a few letters had been received from Norway and Sweden which indicated the signal had carried over Russia. In that great distance it would have skipped down on some parts of the Soviet Union. It was a known fact: the Communists were doing all they could to keep the Gospel from entering their country.

To better understand the principle of radio "jamming," let's set up a hypothetical case:

In one of the larger cities of Russia, a small group of devout Christians huddle in front of an antiquated radio receiver. The time is 1:00 A.M. One of the men pulls a big thick gold watch from his vest pocket and says, "It won't be long now, just a few more minutes."

The man closest to the radio reaches over and turns the off-on dial and adjusts the tuning. The usual rolling sound familiar to shortwave reception indicates the signal is coming a long distance. Everyone holds his breath to catch the first words.

"You are listening to the Overseas Service of the Far East Broadcasting Company coming to you from Manila, Philippines. The following program will be directed to our Russian listeners. We are happy to greet you in the name of ...."

At that moment the room is filled with a deafening roar and a high-pitched screech. The group moves in toward the receiver while another tries to adjust the tuning better. Far in the background the voice can be heard. After the Manila station signs off, good reception is resumed.

With head hanging rather low, the owner of the set turns it off, and the group disperses. They leave the house cautiously and one at a time, lest they be seen and suspected of committing such a crime as listening to a Free World broadcast.

Immediately after World War II, Russia set up powerful jamming stations to interfere with Russian-language broadcasts from America and England. It wasn't long before more than twenty-five hundred different interference stations were counted and locations checked by Free World broadcasters! An all-out effort to blanket all eighty-five Voice of America stations was put forth: they tried to blot out the many frequencies used by VOA.

After the Polish government closed down its jamming stations, it made known some facts: For every dollar spent by the Voice of America, the Polish government spent over one hundred dollars in a vain attempt to keep news and other programming from crossing its international border.

General Gruenther, former chief of NATO, has said that the Communists have spent several billion dollars in their jamming efforts! So powerful and potent are results of broadcasting, the Reds dare not allow the Gospel of Jesus Christ to be preached to their people. They say there is no God; that nobody anymore believes in Him! Therefore, they want to block the broadcasts from the Philippines which tell of a loving heavenly Father and His Son, Jesus Christ, and ignore the fact that Christians outside the iron curtain countries *do believe in Him.*

There are several reasons why the Communists do not jam as badly as they did at first. It is known now that jamming is only about 50 percent effective. Listeners still hear, but with difficulty. The cost is prohibitive! The Communists are telling themselves the Gospel broadcasts are not effective; that nothing is happening to their people because of listening. Basically, the fight against Communism is a spiritual warfare. When the truth of the Gospel gets through, men's lives are changed. And they don't want that to happen.

For weeks the engineers at Christian Radio City were aware of their signal being jammed. In a letter from one of their Russian program suppliers, he suggested music as the answer. Russians love music, and after giving this a try for awhile, they found even Gospel hymns were not being jammed. Then it was suggested that very short Gospel messages be interspersed with the music. But the Reds were on their toes! Almost the very instant any speaking came on, the deafening roar blocked out the Gospel message. When the speaking went off, the jamming ceased.

For weeks, the programs that came out of Christian Radio City were made up of light symphony music. Right in the middle of a number, there would be a quick break, with a verse of Scripture given by the Russian announcer! As many times as not, the man at the jamming station switch would not get the jammer turned on in time. But the problem was only partially licked! FEBC needed far more powerful transmitters to penetrate that electronic iron curtain! Some Voice of America stations had to be increased to one million watts in order to override the jamming stations!

Not only Russian broadcasts were being jammed: Peking had to do something about the Gospel getting into China. It wasn't long until the China releases over FEBC, primarily news programs, were jammed as badly as the Russian broadcasts.

Jamming is not only expensive but a highly complicated job. The general technique takes the form of superimposing buzz-saw-like noises upon the identical frequency of the offending station. It being impossible to set up the jamming station near the offending station—like Manila—the jammer is built near each large city capable of receiving signals from the offender. Each time programming comes through, the jammer receives the signal on a common radio receiver like those in homes. As soon as offending programming is received, the jamming station switch is turned and the "bagpipes" start playing! Only rarely does the jamming station impose its own program over the other. A radio engineer's ear can quickly catch the sound of a jammer.

Because of medium wave and shortwave, daytime and night broadcasts, each has to be dealt with individually. Therefore, to the jammer, the headaches must be numerous, and the job expensive!

Especially in shortwave jamming—which is the most frequent and potent—the offending signal has been beamed to a target area. Therefore, the jamming stations in that area must go into action. But, in shortwave broadcasts, there is often a splatter of signals. If the offending programs are getting through to other cities, the Communists have a network of stations—as we have in America—and these local broadcast stations have to be converted instantly from their own propaganda programs to a jamming signal. This is very costly to the Communists, and a dead giveaway that they do not want the Truth to be broadcast to their people, for what else can they think when a local station switches from a program to high-pitched noises!

Special transmitters for jamming operations have been developed by Soviet engineers. These machines are designed for rapid frequency shifting and are capable of heavy noise signals and often fill a band of five or six kilocycles each side of the offending frequency. Jamming transmitters of this type are known to have power levels up to one million watts.

By some shifts in time, frequencies, and program material, many jamming stations were caught off guard and the programming from Christian Radio City got into Russia and China! Down through the centuries, enemies of the Cross of Jesus Christ have tried to suppress His teachings, destroy His written Word and persecute anyone who follows Him.

> For all flesh is as grass, and all the glory of man as the
> flower of grass;
> The grass withereth, and the flower thereof falleth
> away,
> BUT THE WORD OF THE LORD ENDURETH FOREVER.

Man was not created in the form of a machine. He is capable of thinking and reasoning. Through heaviness caused by sin, he naturally yearns for peace. The Word of God, as it falls on the ear of a person for the first time, usually puts a hunger within him. "This is it! This is what I want," his heart cries. And to the child of God, whether in fellowship with the Lord or backslidden, there comes a strengthening when he hears the Words of Life. Such is the way it affects radio listeners in all lands. The two letters that follow are from listeners in Russia and China. Both names and addresses are withheld to guard against their persecution.

Northeast China

DEAR PASTOR AND COMRADES IN THE GOSPEL MINISTRY:

Peace to you—I do not write for anything. I am a Christian. My name is .... I am now working in .... cooperative as one who tends the stock and also as a watchman. My home is in .... My native country is .... Before the redistribution of land, there was a church in my village. After the re-

distribution in 1949, the church was changed into a
school. I was then discouraged. For fourteen years I
have been cut off from communication with the church.
Lately I am assigned to this job. I listen to Gospel broadcast. Thank the Lord who gives me a chance to return
to the bosom of Jesus, to be close to Him. In the Lord
I listen to the voice of pastor and preacher and have
spiritual fellowship with the Lord. I live with my wife
who is a Christian, my daughter and her husband and
child. Two families—five persons live together. In order to help my daughter to believe in the Lord I need a
copy of the catechism and a copy of the Gospel notes.
I hope, pastor, you will mail them to me. I won't write
about other things now.

> May God bless you.
> Your brother in the Lord,
> (signed) . . . .

*   *   *   *

Eastern Russia

DEAR BROTHERS—

I, as the least brother, ..., like to greet you in
the name of our Lord Jesus Christ, who has loved us
with eternal love.

I am often listening to your messages over the radio.
My heart fills with overflowing joy that the Lord privi-
leged you for this call and the whole world is hearing
the message of our Lord Christ. It is written the Gospel shall be preached in all the world for a witness.

It's the desire of my heart that you may remember
Ephesians 5:2.

Dear brothers, please, reply to my petition. You are
telling over the radio [broadcasting] [the listeners] may
get such free of charge. I am ready to obtain even for
pay. I beg you earnestly if only possible.

> Good-by. May God help you for success!
> Your spiritual brother,
> (signed) . . . .

Chapter Ten

THE WHYS AND WHEREFORES

THE THAI FARMER far up in the riverlands, the Burmese government official, the Indonesian clerk, the Ilongot headhunter, the fierce Moro tribesman, the Filipino student, the Hong Kong merchant, the lonely leper on Palawa, the sufferer in a Taiwan hospital, the Ceylon plantation worker, the GI stationed at one of the United States arsenals of defense in the Far East, the Japanese teen-ager, the seaman on the Indian Ocean, the Tibetan trader at the top of the world, the white Russian behind the iron curtain, the Chinese Christian behind the bamboo curtain—how else could all these people and many more be reached, except by the invasive means of RADIO!

Probably 95 percent of the people who read these pages could not tell a condenser from a resistor, and most of them couldn't care less. And yet, in the preceding nine chapters we have been telling of the results of radio without telling what it is. At this point, the author is reluctant to display his ignorance, for alas, he too is one of the 95 percent!

Thinking in generalities, the average housewife, clerk, farmer, or businessman in America does not give the mechanics of radio much thought. For years it has been a part of his or her life. Most of us have grown up with it.

One eminent scientist said, "Radio was not invented, it was discovered." Just as the laws of gravity were discovered, so the laws of radio were unfolded. Radio has been here all the time—since creation!

As we have driven across the country, many of us have

had the experience of noticing our hometown radio station gradually fading away until we could get only a very faint signal with the volume on full. Then we flipped the dial until we were able to pick up a station from the city miles ahead of us. As we approached the city, the signal increased to its maximum and then gradually faded away as we continued on our cross-country trip. The question which has come to many minds at this point is: Since I can't pick up a station from very far away, how can one broadcast from Manila to Africa, India and Russia?

Probably the biggest reason why this is a problem to many Americans is because shortwave radios are almost an unheard-of piece of living room furniture. Years ago, before the advent of TV, many of the radios had one, two or even three bands of shortwave. But in America, with its thousands of newspapers and excellent coverage of news by local radio stations, the shortwave bands vanished from our dials. However, in most other lands of the world today this is not the case. Multiplied millions of people the world over depend on their shortwave radio for news coverage as well as for general programs. *There are many more radio receivers in the world than there are copies of daily newspapers printed each day.*

Second, many governments own and control all the radio stations within their respective nations. Therefore, listeners are obliged to swallow only what the government decides to feed them; unless, of course, they have shortwave and can listen to a broadcast from another country. Americans do not realize that countless hours are spent by multitudes round the world listening to shortwave reception.

To continue our nontechnical description of shortwave radio, we go all the way back to creation. God planned from eternity that the world be enclosed in a gaseous envelope, like a cantaloupe suspended in a plastic bag. Approximately forty miles out in space begins what is known as the ionosphere, and this continues on to about four hundred miles, changing in its position during the twenty-four-hour period of the day. This ionosphere is made up of layers, and is ionized by the ultraviolet rays of the sun.

Our local radio stations are known as AM (Amplitude Modulation, whatever that means!), and the signal falls off rapidly. FM and TV signals follow the line of sight and leave the earth at the horizon to go off into space. However, short-wave signals shoot toward the sky, and since the ionosphere acts like a giant mirror, they are reflected or bounced back to earth, where they are reflected back to the ionosphere and back to earth, and so on—following the curvature of the earth.

Since there is more than one layer in the ionosphere, some of the signal pierces through to the second and third layers (each representing a sharper angle up), and returns to earth closer than the signal reaching only the first layer.

As the signal hits the earth on its return from the iono-sphere, it splatters like a bucket of roof paint accidentally spilled. Since radio engineers are able to calculate on paper where they want the signal to go, the ionosphere cooperates in returning the waves back to earth to the "target area." The splatter includes a large area. Therefore, a whole coun-try like Thailand, Japan, India, or Korea would be included in the target area. Whole countries like Russia and China would not be reached in the first "splatter" but might have three or more such "dips."

God, in His all-wise foresight and knowledge, created the earth with this layer of ionosphere. Scientists know of no other value it may have to the world than to bounce short-wave signals back to earth. How else could the multitudes in many lands hear the Gospel other than by shortwave radio? How else could people living behind the iron and bamboo curtains hear unless the signals of shortwave were sent up to the ionosphere and bounced back to earth beyond the international boundaries which keep foreign missionaries without?

With the earth's population increasing by the millions each year, shortwave radio is truly a God-given means to reach the masses with the Gospel. Dare we speculate that the Great Commission can be fulfilled in our day by broadcasting the Gospel to every kindred, tongue, people, and nation?

> The heavens declare the glory of God; and the firmament sheweth his handiwork.
>
> Day unto day uttereth speech, and night unto night sheweth knowledge.
>
> There is no speech nor language, where their voice is not heard.
>
> Their line is gone out through all the earth, and their words to the end of the world.
>
> —Psalm 19:1-4

Chapter Eleven

TO THE REGIONS BEYOND

WHILE ARMOR PLATE and gun mounts were being fitted to airplanes of war, a small Piper Cub at Christian Radio City was used to carry Portable Missionaries to different parts of the Philippines much faster than by surface means.

Billy and Janie Reames, who had arrived in Manila sometime before, were challenged with the need of distributing more PM's. Billy was in charge of extension work. Being a pilot, Janie used her Piper Cub to haul these radios to places where it would have taken days to go any other way. However, there was a problem! Janie was so small she couldn't start her own airplane. Not having an electric starter, it had to be "propped" by hand, and that was one job she couldn't handle. Consequently, she had to keep the engine running when she landed or be sure there was a man around who could do the job.*

* * * *

Day and night, hundreds of radio transmitters in Russia, Red China, and eastern Europe viciously discharged the Communists' "big lie." The broadcasts were sent out in a growing effort to sell the Soviet propaganda to people from the vast treeless plains of Argentina to the rice paddies of Thailand.

The Communist radio output totaled 1,240 weekly broadcast hours. The Communists devoted the greatest proportion of their total psychological warfare appropriations to the radio war. They knew what tool was the most effective.

---

*Because of very high maintenance costs, the plane was not used over a lengthy period, but it did help distribute many Portable Missionaries. FEBC was not prepared to expedite the PM ministry by this means.

Five hundred million dollars were appropriated annually by Soviet Russia for its radio war against the principles of godly truth and righteousness! Yet, after nineteen centuries of preaching Christ, many millions of the world's population have not heard the name of Jesus.

The effective radiated power of all transmitters in Christian Radio City amounted to 81,700 watts. This was a dribble compared with what was needed to effectively proclaim the truth to the millions of Asia.

> Thrust in thy sickle, and reap:
> For the time is come for thee to reap;
> For the harvest of the earth is ripe.

The hearts of the directors, Broger, Bowman, and Roberts, were stirred to action! Contracts were signed for two new 10,000-watt transmitters to be built by one of the leading radio companies of America. These new units would boost FEBC's voice to the effective radiated power of 262,500 watts.

The contract called for a total of $74,184.00 for the two transmitters. God had sent in $53,000.00 the first year to launch this sacred ministry to the world. By faith they would believe God to meet this new need.

For weeks, Byrd Brunemeier worked on the construction of the DZI6 transmitter, and then, on October 25, 1952, at 4:00 P.M. all of the personnel who could momentarily leave their tasks gathered to thank the Lord for this new "voice" in the Orient and to dedicate it to the Lord as it formally hit the air waves, joining with its six sister stations in the opening theme, "All hail the power of Jesus' name!"

With seven transmitters lined up against the wall and two new larger ones to come, a new transmitter building was the only answer. Work was started in early 1953 on a quonset-type building forty feet by one hundred feet in size.

In the meantime thrilling letters continued to pour in from other countries.

A missionary from India wrote that he went hunting near the Tibetan border on his vacation. On a number of occasions he met Tibetan traders who, upon seeing that he was a Westerner, approached him asking, "Will you tell us about this Jesus we've been hearing about on the radio?" There was only one place where these men could hear that Name, and that was from Manila!

Understanding some of the Indian languages because of their trading activities, the missionary was able to deal with them and point them to Christ.

A letter came from a man of Chiengmai Province, which is far up in the mountains of northern Thailand. He told how he and a friend had been listening to FEBC's broadcasts. They had never seen a preacher or Christian. About three months later he wrote again, stating that his wife and friend and three other couples had accepted Christ as their personal Saviour. They wondered where the nearest Christian pastor was, that they might be baptized and start a church in their village.

A Muslim, who spoke the Thai language, wrote, saying, "I have been listening to the broadcasts from Manila, and I hear that you have a course that I can get by mail to study the Bible. I wonder if you would be so kind as to send me the necessary information." For months that man regularly sent his lessons on the Gospel of John. He was apparently a man originally from Thailand who was stationed in Mecca, the very heart of the Muslim faith—studying the Gospel of John because he had heard the message through the FEBC stations in Manila!

Max Atienza was the Administrative Director of the work in the Philippines, along with doing considerable broadcasting. One of his programs was at 7:00 A.M. on Sunday in the Tagalog language. He had been doing this release for a long time but did not fully realize what were the results of such a program. Max had an occasion to visit the island of Mindoro and he heard about a village of Nangyan tribesmen who listened to FEBC. These seminomadic people have a very low level of culture. When Max heard they were listening to his program, he was curious and determined to visit them while he was on the island. What he saw completely overwhelmed him.

They had a meeting while he was with them because they wanted him to speak in person. When they started the service, he could hardly believe what he heard.

A man stood up in front of the people who had gathered for the meeting and said, "You are tuned to the stations of the Far East Broadcasting Company, DZAS, DZB2 and DZH6. The time is seven o'clock." From this point they went on with their meeting in a normal manner.

These primitive people had one of the PM's and had listened faithfully to Max every Sunday morning. They had no pastor or teacher; they had no education. Since the program was preceded by a station break and a time check, they assumed that this was the way to start a Gospel service!

Another interesting account comes from Thailand: A missionary paddled his small boat as far as he could go up one of the larger rivers in the northern part of the country, distributing Gospel literature to the villagers. When he came to the mud flats and could not go farther, he turned around to make the long journey back to his mission station. But, as he turned, he spotted a tiny hut on the bank of the river. Not wanting to pass up an opportunity, he paddled over to the bank below the hut and climbed out to greet the Thai farmer. "What brings you up here?" the Thai called to the foreign missionary.

"I have come to bring you a witness of the true God."

Then the farmer surprised him by saying, "Oh, do you have a copy of God's holy Word?"

The missionary replied, "How did you know about God's holy Word?"

The old farmer, far from the last reaches of civilization, said, "Oh, I've been listening to a broadcast in the Thai language, and the broadcaster has told me to get a copy of God's holy Word at my earliest convenience. Do you have one?"

The missionary held up his copy and the old man got so excited, he clapped his hands for joy, for it was the very first time he had seen a copy of the Word of God.

Another thrilling report comes from high in the mountains of Central Laos:

Three days by foot and horseback from the main road is the village of Ben Pho Sang Noy. The people are Meo—tribesmen from China who speak Lao. Ben Pho Sang Nay has a church, a congregation, but no pastor! This is typical, for there are two hundred villages in this mountainous country, about eight thousand Christians in all, but only fourteen Christian workers to minister to them.

The church at Ben Pho Sang Noy has the distinction of having for its minister—a RADIO!

The people are very poor, but Mr. Bah Khu, a rice farmer and Christian, has a radio in his home, and into this humble dwelling the people of the church crowd to hear the radio preach to them in their own tongue. Nearly every night they listen to the broadcasts beamed from Manila. This church would have no minster if Bah Khu had no radio—and if miracles through the gifts of His people had not provided the stations of FEBC in Manila—and if consecrated Christian workers were unwilling to put a lot of time into recording radio programs!

Putting these programs together is not easy. This is the way it is done: once every three months, "Gus" Gustafson, pastor of the church at Vientiane, Laos, leaves his station along with workers who will assist with the programs. The first part of the trip is by air; then, traveling by bus, by dug-out canoe, and again by bus, they arrive at Udorn, Thailand. All the next day is spent on the train to Korat, where the Paul Johnson memorial studios are located. (This studio also supplies FEBC with Thai language tapes.) Arriving about the same time will be Armand Heineger, Swiss missionary, from Savannakhet. He has spent two or three days on his trip. First he has to ferry his car across the Mekong River, balancing it precariously on two dugout canoes. He drives all day, sleeping when too tired to drive farther. Later in the evening of the second day or on the morning of the third, he arrives in Korat with his party.

About ten days are required to record the programs necessary to fill the radio schedule for the next three months. A good part of the recording is done in the manner called "Lum Lao." This combines music and story-telling with Scripture and poetry in a traditional style utterly indigenous to the Lao people. It is something for which they will stop most anything to enjoy.

Because of the serious shortage of Christian workers to minister to the many villagers, the broadcasts alternate between evangelistic, devotional, and Bible teaching. Thus, the radio serves as actual pastor as well as evangelist. Many Lao have followed Christ. Many have done it in response to the invitation to Christ heard from the voice of the Reverend Radio!

Chapter Twelve

COINCIDENCE OR DIVINE
PLAN?

THE CONTRACT for the two 10,000-watt transmitters being built in the east called for a monthly payment of $2,000.00. Several installments had been made, plus the $8,000.00 downpayment. Then, a letter came from the transmitter company demanding they remain in the United States in a bonded warehouse until final payment was made! That meant, at the rate they were being paid for, they couldn't be shipped to the Philippines for over *two years*.

Pages could be written on the struggle that followed, but few people would care to wade through that kind of reading material! Money was slow in coming in. The home staff took a cut of 20 percent in their salaries to help in this emergency.

The first big transmitter had been built and delivered to a west coast warehouse. By March, 1954, only $20,100.00 had come in for the payment of the first unit.

In May, Mr. Roberts was conducting a service in a church on the west coast. During the meeting he mentioned the fact that $12,000.00 was urgently needed to finish paying for the first transmitter and that if this could be done and the transmitter shipped before July, a saving of $1,300.00 could be made on import duty alone.

At the close of the service, a young man, John Ross, who had been a Christian less than six months, came to him and said, "Mr. Roberts, I want to loan the Far East Broadcasting Company $12,000.00 so that transmitter can be released for shipment immediately instead of standing in the warehouse until November."

Astonished, Roberts said, "What interest do you want?"

"No interest. I want to do it for the Lord. I wish I could make it a gift but I can't right now. But, if you can pay me back at the same rate you are paying the transmitter company, I will make the loan at no interest," he answered.

Just the possibility of shipping the first transmitter was cause for great rejoicing, but it entailed the immediate responsibility for freight to Manila and duty upon arrival. The duty was thought to be 30 percent of the total cost of the transmitter!

Besides the tremendous cost of shipping, duty, and installation of the first, the second transmitter had been delivered to the west coast warehouse and could not be released until the remaining $25,000.00 was paid. Not only were interest charges piling up but the storage bill was no small item!

Don and Helen Smith had arrived in Christian Radio City sometime before. Don was a busy man when the transmitter arrived in seventeen boxes and needed to be carefully unpacked and checked. Being in charge of the electronic department, he had to keep the other units humming. Bob Reynolds, who had been working with FEBC out of the home office, had accompanied the big transmitter to Manila and worked with the others to get it on the air by September, 1954.

* * * *

With so many Chinese having streamed into Formosa from the mainland, a golden opportunity existed for broadcasting to these refugees and to military personnel.

It was decided that Dick Rowland would take over the Formosa project, and it wasn't long before they had a studio set up in Taipei. Being able to purchase time on local stations at a ridiculously low rate—$1.20 for each broadcast hour—they were soon operating 292 hours each month over five Formosan transmitters. Another 218 hours were made available to them at the same rates, but the budget would not allow it! From Taipei also came tapes for the Chinese releases over the Manila transmitters.

* * * *

As the last payment on the loan was turned over to John Ross, he happened to say, "How are you making out on the second transmitter you expect to ship over to Manila?"

Roberts paused, then with slight hesitation answered, "I believe . . . yes, I'm sure we still owe about $12,000.00."

"That's a coincidence," Ross said. "That was what you needed to get the first ones moving, and now that same amount will get the second underway." He agreed to loan the same money on the same terms to release the second one for immediate shipment!

Just eight months before, Ross had loaned the money needed to clear the first 10,000-watt transmitter, and now he was willing to loan the same money the second time!

Roberts looked up with a smile on his face and said, "You know, this will save us $625.00 in interest and considerable in storage fees, and get the transmitter on the air six months sooner."

* * * *

Paul Belles, a Christian who was employed by an electronic corporation in the northwest manufacturing testing equipment, mainly oscilloscopes, learned of the work of the Far East Broadcasting Company. Later, when Bob Bowman was in a meeting in that area, Mr. Belles became more interested, and urgings of the Spirit which he had begun to feel were confirmed. He felt led of the Lord to obtain one of those costly and valuable oscilloscopes for the FEBC stations in Manila.

Belles had already launched this project when the FEBC home office received a list of badly needed electronic equipment from Manila. The $4,500.00 transmitter fund had to be paid off before they could expect to get any of the items on the list—and one thing they needed badly was an oscilloscope! "And it shall come to pass, that before they call, I will answer" (Isa. 65:24).

Through the cooperation of his company, Belles was able to locate a cathode-ray oscilloscope in the east for $350.00—original price, $950.00. Eighteen fellow workers and three outsiders helped Belles purchase this instrument, and the company put it in first-class shape. Flying Tiger Airline flew the delicate instrument to Whittier, California, where the home office crated it for shipment overseas. (To non-technically minded people, such as most of us are, this requires an explanation to share the enthusiasm of the technical men for this complicated bit of machinery. In essence, its function, when placed on any of the eight transmitters of the FEBC stations, is to quickly and accurately pinpoint difficulties which otherwise might cost the technicians hours of troublesome labor to locate, while the signal would continue to go out faulty.)

To Belles, Operation Oscilloscope meant the joy of hearing the voice of the Spirit of God and being able to respond.

To listeners in the Orient, it meant a clearer, more perfect Gospel signal through the air waves. A trumpet with a distinct sound.

> And even things without life giving sound, whether pipe or harp, except they give a distinction in the sounds, how shall it be known what is piped or harped? For if the trumpet give an uncertain sound, who shall prepare himself to the battle? (I Corinthians 14:7-8).

This is a typical FEBC story, typical of the many times God has shown He is not limited by man's extremities.

* * * *

Richard Bronson had been a member of the FEBC family from its beginning. Having had experience in business management, he had kept the home office running smoothly. But the day came when he and his family were able to head for Manila for a term of service as general director.

Before World War II, the Bronsons were missionaries in eastern Europe. For a number of years they worked among Slavic people. During that time he learned enough of the Russian language to be able to converse in a limited manner.

As soon as the first overseas transmitter was operational in Manila, Bronson urged the use of Russian language broadcasts, and they were some of the first released on a regular schedule.

As Richard Bronson tells it, "I saw the Communists jamming our signal more and more, until our engineers were able to count as high as eight jammers zeroing in on our 10,000-watt voice. Although the jamming was very serious, still, because of technical reasons, it was only about 50 percent effective. The signal went through and could be heard by those who wanted to listen. It was during this period when jamming was so bad I wondered if it was worth it all.

"At this point, I was considering asking the program department to take off the Russian programs entirely and use that time for more Chinese releases because it is the largest language block in the world. It is said that one out of every four is a Chinese. We were praying to know if we should cut out the Russian and concentrate more heavily on Chinese.

"One afternoon, our daughter, Kay, fell and broke her ankle and had to be taken to the hospital in the south side of Manila. After we were finished at the hospital, we started back toward the city of Manila intending to drive through it, but as we approached the heavy traffic, I told Marge I just couldn't fight that traffic again. I had been in the city three times that day and didn't feel up to an hour of working my way between and around 'all twenty thousand' jeepneys!*

"We decided to turn round and go to Christian Radio City, which is north of Manila, via the circumferential drive. Because of the extreme heat and high humidity, Marge felt faint and suggested we stop and get some coffee. The nearest place was the Manila international airport. We stopped there.

"Upon entering the airport restaurant, we discovered fifty or sixty European people and, having been so accustomed to seeing black-haired Filipinos, we were completely astounded. Men were wearing heavy wool suits with baggy pants and vests, while the women wore babushka shawls.

"My first thought was that they were probably Hungarian refugees being repatriated out in the Orient, since it was near the end of the Hungarian uprising. But as we sat down at a small table and pulled ours as close as we could to theirs, we discovered they were speaking Russian. Then, I was all the more concerned as to where all these Russians came from!

"Trying to strike up a conversation with an elderly couple, I had little success since we had been away from actual ministry with Russians for so long. Finally, I asked the elderly lady if she could speak German—thinking I could do better with that language. She said, 'Na, vee no speak German, vee no speak English, vee Russians.'

"At that moment a young man about twenty-five years old came over and sat with the elderly couple and told us in very poor English that they were his grandparents and that the whole group were on their way to *freedom*. And he said that with a great deal of emphasis! Then he added that they were from Manchuria and were on their way to Australia.

*Small buses made from worn-out World War II jeeps. There are still many thousands in use.

"To try to converse any further was no use; he just couldn't understand my English and I couldn't understand him. Finally, our conversation degenerated down to my counting from one to twenty in Russian and saying a dozen or more phrases in Russian that I could remember. Then he counted to twenty in English and said a few expressions.

"It came time for them to leave and proceed by plane to their destination. Most of them were getting up and making ready to leave the room. At that moment, I thought of one more phrase—it was 'Slova Bosia,' which means something like 'Praise God!'

"I wish you could have seen the look on their faces! That young fellow jumped from his chair, and the elderly couple beamed from ear to ear as they looked with astonishment at us. The young man pointed to the ceiling and hallooed, 'Slova Bosia, Slova Bosia,' then turned to me and pointed to his own chest and cried out, 'I also! I also!' At that very moment we realized we were brothers in Christ!

"That young man ran round among those people and gathered together about ten of them and came back to us. We found they too were Christians. When they learned we were Christians, they could hardly believe it because they had been told by the Communists for years that nobody anymore believed in a God. The excitement was tremendous. Although we could not make each other understood, tears began to flow down their cheeks. The little old lady was down on her knees and had her arms round Marge's legs. And the little old man was searching in his pockets and finally came out with a Russian stamp and gave it to Kay as a souvenir.

"Just then a big, fine-looking Russian came over and, in perfect English, said he had been secretary of the YMCA in Harbin, Manchuria and asked if I were from a radio station in Manila. I said, 'Yes.'

"Then he asked, 'Do you broadcast the evangelical religion in Russian?'

"I answered that we did, and he questioned further, 'On twenty-five meters?'

"I said, 'Yes, we sure do!'

"He replied, 'Well, friend, we have been listening to you for years. You have been the only contact we have had with Christians on the outside.'

"'Fine!' I said. 'That is marvelous, but what about the jamming? Don't they jam our signal something terrible?'

"'Oh, yes,' he said, 'the jamming! But, you know, this young fellow you have been talking to took an ordinary radio and converted it to 25 meters. We would go to his home in the middle of the night—two or three at a time— lest we be suspected, sit on the floor, cover our heads with a blanket, divide a set of headphones so that several could listen at one time, and try to hear some message of hope and encouragement from the outside world.' He continued. 'That jamming almost drove us crazy, but you know, it was worth it all if we could only hear just one word, the Name of Jesus, or just one verse of Scripture. It was worth it all! Then we knew that faith wasn't dead; that there were Christians on the outside who believe in God and maybe were praying for us!'

"Almost beside myself with joy, I found we were walking out the gate together, but the customs officers were holding me back from going on out to the plane. As the crowd kept walking slowly toward the transport, the big fellow yelled back, 'Continue the broadcasts. There are many thousands of Russians listening to that broadcast and depending on your message of hope.'

"The farther out he got, the louder he yelled. 'The Communists don't realize the finest Gospel propaganda is in the hymns of the church. Continue to broadcast the music. They don't jam it at all. Don't stop broadcasting. There are many depending on it. Make it as late at night as you can. God bless you!'

"In a few minutes the door of the DC-6 was closed, the stairs rolled away, propellers were turning, and the plane taxied to the end of the runway.

"This had all happened in less than fifteen minutes! Now it seemed like a dream. We couldn't believe such a thing had happened!

"Later that day I checked with the Philippine Military Intelligence and the American Embassy and no one knew of any Russian refugees going through Manila that day! Not a single newsman or photographer was there to get a story. No one had known of the flight! And yet the Lord caused us to be there at that very time to be encouraged that the Russian broadcasts were going through. You can be sure we didn't take the Russian programs off the air. We increased them instead.

"Sometime after these refugees arrived in Australia they wrote stating they had been in Communist Chinese territory. Russians in Chinese country didn't set well with the Chinese leaders. They wanted to get rid of them because of all the food they were eating and the jobs they were taking away from the Chinese. As long as they left Manchuria, it didn't matter to the Chinese which way they went—east or west.

"The Russian government bid high for them to return to their homeland. Promises of good jobs, lots of food, and everything wonderful were made to them; but the choice was theirs. If they had an invitation from any country, they were free to leave. Some went to Australia, some to Canada, and some to South America. But a few fell for the promises made by the Russians and returned to their native land, never to be heard from again. But before they parted, they all agreed to listen each night to the Russian broadcast coming from Christian Radio City, Manila—those in Australia, those in Canada, those in Russia (if they were able to listen), and those in South America. And they would have fellowship together in the Gospel through the radio even though they were separated by thousands of miles.

"Let me tell you, this experience made me tingle from head to foot!"

Chapter Thirteen

THE BATIA CRISIS

BATIA HAD BEEN A PEACEFUL COMMUNITY before Communist aggression forced it to make a major decision. The men were pressured to either bear arms against the struggling Philippine government or turn their farming settlement into a food supply center for the Reds. The latter choice was made.

Submarines from unknown ports were landing small arms in remote bays after dark. The Philippine Islands had become the target for invasive Communist action. By day the whole countryside took on an innocent appearance as if everyone were working hard to rebuild their war-torn country. A casual visitor might not have suspected any trouble existed. But the picture changed after sundown. The Huks would sweep down from the hills and rule certain parts of the country with the muzzle of a gun.

But for some strange reason the villagers of Batia did not join ranks with the fighting Huks who were working their way closer to the city of Manila. Other barrios either cooperated or they were constantly ravaged. Food was a problem to the roving Huks. To supplement their plundering, they needed a steady supply of their staple food—rice. Batia was not the richest farming area but it usually had a good crop of rice and vegetables in season.

So strong was the Communist action in the days of 1949 and 1950 that few people had much confidence left in their government. The Communists had even gone so far as to set up universities in the jungles. "Stalin universities" were held in an impregnable forest high on the slopes of Mt. Arayat, about eighty miles north of Manila. Here the Reds taught Filipino youth their system of world domination. At each important road junction, machine-gun nests ruled the highways at night. Only the bravest souls traveled after sundown. Few people realized how close the Philippines came to falling into the Communists' hands in those days.

Ramon Magsaysay had been appointed as Secretary of Defense by President Quirino. Almost singlehandedly he accepted the challenge of freeing his beloved land from the impending danger of Communism. His first mission was the most dangerous. Armed with only a six-gun, he traveled by Piper Cub to the barrios, often landing in a cow pasture, visiting the villagers and trying to win their confidence. Disregarding the danger to his life, he gave speeches in public gatherings where Huks were in attendance. But because of the binding grip held by the Reds during the night hours, something more than words had to be used to win this battle!

Before sundown on April 7, trucks towing light artillery were seen moving slowly down the highway not far from Batia. This was not an uncommon thing since the government was trying to do all it could to stop the Huks, but most action had not been fruitful to date. Little did the villagers know the big trucks and guns had stopped beside the road and were waiting behind the bamboo clumps about five hundred yards away.

As usual, that evening the Huks swarmed in from the countryside to carry food supplies to their bases in the foothills. Without warning, the government cannon belched forth its deadly shells and spewed shrapnel in the center of the village. Screams of pain were heard from the unprotected passersby. It wasn't long before small fires started burning uncontrollably. But to add to the confusion, the big guns kept hammering away.

Lights were put out, but it was too late now. Flimsy bamboo houses were burning as if they were matchboxes. As shells exploded, cries of pain were heard from wounded Filipinos. The night was long and agonizing; much property had been destroyed.

As soon as the first rays of sun started to peep over the hills, families whose houses were still standing brought their dead outside. Twelve covered bodies lay on a porch of one of the larger dwellings.

*　*　*　*

One of the men of Batia, Feliciano Cristobal, had been listening to his radio weeks before. Without fail, each evening, he had his ear near the speaker. What was this new propaganda he was hearing? It couldn't be Communism—or was it a subtle way for them to present their lies? This new way promised peace—the thing he longed for— through the life of a Man, Jesus Christ.

Communism had made numerous promises. But this voice on the radio spoke of a personal joy and happiness. It almost sounded too good to be true. Not allowing anything to distract him from that evening broadcast, Feliciano listened with a heart warmed by the possibility of his load of sin being taken by the very Son of God. One night the voice said, "Will you come to Jesus as you are, let Him cleanse your heart from sin, and make you a new man?" The voice continued with a verse from the Bible: "If any man be in Christ, he is a new creature. Old things are passed away. Behold, all things are become new."

Young Feliciano Cristobal, so challenged by the power of the Word, accepted Christ as his personal Saviour. And what a difference it made in his life! Folks in the barrio noticed him and asked one another what had happened. Feliciano's lips couldn't remain silent; he told his closest friends what had happened. Nightly, from that time on, the little radio was the most popular means of diversion. But, listening was not only something to pass the time; it was doing something to the villagers.

Could that be the reason Batia would not bear arms against the government? Young as they were, the few Christians, whose lives had been so changed, were a strong influence on the other villagers.

*   *   *   *

About four months after that dreadful shelling experience, six young men made their way from Batia to Christian Radio City in Manila. As they approached the buildings from the road, carrying their bedrolls and rice, they looked as though they were coming to stay awhile—and that was exactly what they had in mind. These young Christians wanted to learn more about the Christ they had recently accepted. Specifically, they wanted training in soul-winning!

The men were permitted to stay at Christian Radio City where they were given training by representatives of different Bible schools in the Manila area. After three weeks of intensive study, they were given diplomas—strictly homemade—in a unique graduation service.

Fired with a vision to return to their barrio and instruct their people in the Word of God, these young firebrands were successful in witnessing and leading other villagers to the Lord.

Nearly eight months later, a letter was received at Christian Radio City from the Christians in Batia. In short it read, "Would Max Atienza come out to Batia?"

Even though the six men who had made their way to Christian Radio City for training in the Word showed every sign of sincerity, Max, who had been the Filipino radio preacher, couldn't erase from his mind the possibility of this being a plot instigated by the Communists. The radio missionaries knew well the potency of the broadcasts. Armed Huks had been active on the road leading into Christian Radio City. Everyone knew the Huks would confiscate the transmitters first if an all-out invasion were made of the

capital. Or the Reds would seek to destroy the stations so
that the populace could not be warned of impending danger.

For months the radio missionaries felt keenly the dangerous situation they were facing. Retreat was not considered. As never before the Filipinos needed to hear the truth,
and radio was the most effective means of reaching out to
the barrios. Yet, they felt every move was being watched.
Without giving vent to their feelings, each one of the engineers had privately wondered what would be the best plan
should the Huks rush in upon the station to take over. Should
they immediately destroy it themselves or let the Huks have
it? On the door of each building they stapled a note written in English and Tagalog* saying that the personnel were
American and stating the Christian purpose of the station.

Max prayed for guidance about going to Batia but was
reluctant to make such a journey, especially since he remembered Batia had been chosen as the barrio which was shelled
by the Philippine government. If he only knew what was
really going on out there!

Taking his young son, Isaac, with him, he started down the
road in a jeep toward Batia. Max couldn't make himself
drive fast. He would have been happy for some excuse to
turn around and return.

The closer he got to Batia the more frightened he became.
Within a short distance of the barrio, he decided he couldn't
go through with it and started to turn around in the road.
But it was too late; he had been followed by some of the
villagers! The only thing to do now was proceed. He had
been trapped!

Arriving in the open area of the central part of the barrio,
Max brought the jeep to a stop. Batians started walking
toward him from every quarter. Nothing was said. Max
tried several times to get a conversation started. No success!
Old men stood with arms folded, just watching and waiting.

*The national language.

Max thought, "Whatever they are going to do, I wish they would get it over with!"

Try as he might he couldn't get anyone to talk. His words bounced back as if hitting a brick wall. Finally an old man walked forward and handed Max a piece of paper with two questions written on it. Max was floored when he read it:

1. Is it true that FEBC is a Communist front?
2. If it is true, why does the government allow it to continue to operate?

"What makes you think we are a Communist front? We are anti-Communist," Max excitedly replied.

Then one of the older men opened the conversation. "When the Communists first came to tell us of a better way of life, they gave us many promises. They have not kept a single promise. And the night the government came to shell our barrio, the Huks were the first to run to the hills and left us villagers to face the shelling. We have been listening and hearing all the wonderful promises on the radio, and are wondering if they can be true, or if this could be another way for the Communists to gain our confidence. We want to hear you tell us in person what we have been hearing on the radio."

This was all Max needed to shift into high gear! Opening his Bible, he explained the way of salvation to the large crowd of people.

After this impromptu meeting, Max found that thirty-one of the villagers had been saved through the witness of the six men who had spent the short time at Christian Radio City, and many were listening faithfully to the radio each evening. Because of the interest in spiritual things and the building of a small chapel by the Christians' own hands, the spirit of the Huks had been broken in that area. They had pulled up stakes and left the Batia area.

Like uncontrollable fire, the Gospel message spread

through the homes of Batia and the surrounding country-side. Only through the medium of radio had this fire started burning. Fanned daily by the fresh broadcasts, the embers kept glowing until other fires began. But this is not the end of the Batia story . . .

Chapter Fourteen

OPERATION DISMANTLE

FOR SOME TIME Richard Bronson, who was general manager of the FEBC stations in Manila, had been a close friend of the Undersecretary of National Defense. This young energetic Filipino was busily engaged in five other positions at the same time, several of which were: head of the Psychological Warfare Department, director of Rural Development Program, member of the President's Cabinet, and special advisor to the President. This young man often spent several hours at a time at Christian Radio City and seemed to enjoy talking with members of the staff. Being a broad-minded individual in search of truth, he was not cool to the Gospel as it was presented to him occasionally. Another fine characteristic which marked him was his patriotism and love for his people and his country.

This man should be credited with laying strategic plans for breaking the back of the Communist movement in the Philippine Islands and for the apprehension and incarceration of the top Communist leaders. But one day the Justice Department, pressured by outside influence, was forced to release many of the top Communist leaders because of some legal loopholes which were interpreted as the free right of individuals in a free and democratic nation. Thus, these top-ranking Communists were released on bail, pending further legal procedures.

The Undersecretary of National Defense was very much discouraged by this situation because so many of the fine men of the Philippines, including the President, had jeopardized their lives in getting these troublemaking Communists behind bars.

At this very time, discouraged and broken at what had happened, the Undersecretary drove out to Christian Radio City to talk to Bronson and Atienza. After relating what had happened, the young man's whole being seemed to suggest the feeling, "What's the use—what can be done now?"

Seeing his opportunity, Bronson turned to the official and said, "Well, my friend, you know there is a Higher Power over all situations, and One who can change things as well as change lives."

"I think it is possible to sway the thinking of a mass of people. But an individual—no, I don't think it is possible for a life to be changed."

"Mr. Secretary," Bronson addressed him, "you know the area of Batia and what happened out there one night."

"Yes, how well I remember Batia and what happened there several years ago," interrupted the Undersecretary. "I was in on that shelling. We were positive that place was a Communist stronghold and poured many shells into that barrio during the night from behind the bamboo clumps."

Bronson quickly returned, "May we take you out to Batia and let you talk with some of the people and see what has happened to them? The lives of individuals *and* the whole community have undergone a tremendous change."

"I would surely like to see that, but not today," said the Undersecretary. They took it as a courteous way of dismissing the subject.

However, not many days later, in drove several official cars and jeeps, and out jumped the Undersecretary along with reporters, photographers, bodyguards and chauffeurs. "We're ready to go to Batia!" he exclaimed.

Richard Bronson and Max Atienza accompanied them to the barrio of Batia not many miles north of Christian Radio City. Lest the officials would think the Batians would be influenced by their presence, Bronson and Atienza walked over into a rice paddy and allowed the officials to be alone with the Batians.

The Undersecretary talked with his own people in their language for a long time and could readily see what had happened to them because of the Gospel message they had heard on the radio.

On the way back to Christian Radio City, he said, "You know, fellows, this is one of the most outstanding things I have ever heard. They told me that from one radio and the conversion of one man, Feliciano Cristobal, the thing spread until two years later thirteen churches had started in other barrios nearby, and at their first fellowship conference this summer, over three hundred attended. Some are meeting even in homes. This is fantastic!"

Later that evening he called President Magsaysay* and told him what he had witnessed that day. Late that night, without bodyguards, the President had his chauffeur drive him to the barrio of Batia to see for himself what had happened.

The President of the Philippines could hardly believe his eyes. He saw firsthand what had happened and talked with many villagers concerning their belief. Upon returning to the Capital far past midnight, he called the Undersecretary at his home and said, "This thing is unbelievable. What has happened here we want to happen other places. We must tell this story and give this message to our people. In fact, we must share this with the peoples of Asia. This will change the very course of the Communists. We must do everything we can to help get this story to our people and to the nations round us. Call up the manager of DZAS right away and tell

*From Secretary of Defense he had been elected President, but was later killed in a plane crash. President Magsaysay was held in high esteem by all Filipinos.

him we want to do everything we can to help get this story out."

"But, Mr. President, do you realize what time it is?" the Undersecretary asked.

"It doesn't matter what the hour is. It's time we see some action. I've never seen a change in people like I saw to-night," the President continued.

A few minutes later the intercom rang in the Bronson apartment. Supposing it was one of the engineers with some trouble down in the transmitter building, Bronson grabbed the receiver and yawned out, "Yeah." An urgent phone call was awaiting him in the office.

The perky voice on the other end surprised Bronson by saying ,"Can you come to my home right now? I have some-thing important to speak to you about. I shall be expecting you soon!"

Bronson almost thought it was a dream when he listened to the Undersecretary tell him what the President had said.

*   *   *   *

Some months prior to this, Jim and Doris Copal were on their way to serve as radio missionaries in Manila. As the ship sailed from Los Angeles to San Francisco, Jim saw a huge antenna array. With a few days ashore, they were able to take in some of the sights, but Jim kept thinking of the radio towers and decided to investigate. The antenna array covered over twelve acres and consisted of sixteen main towers, twelve of which were over one hundred eighty feet tall.

Inside the transmitter building were two electronic giants. One was a 50,000-watt RCA transmitter having two radio frequency units making it capable of instantaneous band-switching from one frequency to another. The other was a 100,000-watt GE transmitter. Both front panels were sixty-eight feet long! The power supply occupied one entire vault of the transmitter building. The switch for the equipment stood five feet tall: copper pipe was used instead of wire to run electricity to the switch panel. The plate transformer was ten feet high, weighed eight tons, and held seven hundred fifty gallons of transformer oil!

Jim found out this installation was a part of the international network operated for the Office of War Information and later for Voice of America. When he arrived in Manila he relayed the information back to the home office in Whittier, California.

The United States government had used these stations to broadcast programs in twenty-one different languages— from San Francisco to the Aleutians, all the Orient, Australia and South America. But now they were surplus to government requirements and were up for sale by sealed bids.

From the strength of this information, the Executive Board of FEBC went to San Francisco to make further investigation. They learned that only three days remained before the bids were to be closed in Washington, D.C. The equipment had originally cost over three-quarters of a million dollars. What hope could there be of trying to interest the government in a bid they could afford!

Because of previous commitments, they decided to bid $30,500.00 to be paid over a period of five years, realizing if this equipment could be secured, it would give evangelical Christianity another powerful voice.

The bid was sent to Washington, D.C., to the United States Information Agency.

Then came the time of waiting!

The phone rang one morning. The call came from Washington, D.C. The legal representative of the War Surplus Board expected to be in Los Angeles the following morning and wanted to see Bowman and Roberts!

When he arrived, his first question was, "What in the world possessed you fellows to make such a bid as this?"

Stumbling for an answer, they were too slow, for the man

answered the question for himself. "I suppose it is because your organization is carried on by contributions of interested people."

That seemed like a good answer. Bowman said, "Yes, sir, that is it."

"Do you men know what is really involved in moving that installation out of San Francisco?" he asked.

Roberts interjected, "How long do we have?"

"Well, we wish it were out of there yesterday, because it is costing the government $1,000.00 a month for lease on the land. You will have forty-five days."

That seemed to be all he was interested in, except to warn them of the magnitude of the moving operation.

The next day the phone rang at the FEBC office. It was the same man calling again from the airport just before he embarked for Washington. He said, "I just wanted to ask you once more if you really know what you are getting into."

Bowman casually assented that it would be a big job, but he thought they could handle it.

*   *   *   *

At the same time, the Assistant Chief of Radio Control Division of the Philippine government attended the International Telecommunication Union in Geneva, Switzerland. Upon his return to Manila, he emphatically informed the staff of Christian Radio City as to the results of the conference.

"The Communists," he said, "have refused to accept international control on frequencies above six megacycles. Therefore, from now on, it is the dog with the biggest bark that will be heard."

What did this mean? Only one thing: the Reds would use any frequency they wanted and put as much power on as they felt necessary to gain their purpose. Other broadcasters trying to abide by the international laws would be over-ridden!

*   *   *   *

Finally the answer came. A letter from the Office of War Information, with a contract enclosed, had this sentence which seemed to stand out in bold print: ". . . whereas the bid of contractor was the highest received, and the agency has determined that it would be advantageous to the government to accept same, . . ."

As the FEBC directors returned to San Francisco to start the job of dismantling, they realized God had made the gigantic equipment shrink in their minds when they first saw it, or their faith would have been too small. Now they were seeing it in its true dimensions. The towers were twice as high as they had thought! First impressions were that they were made from two-by-fours, but now they saw they were made out of six-by-sixes! The transmitters were many times bigger than they had first conceived. All but pinching themselves, they had to come to a quick realization that all the equipment and towers had to be removed—and the grounds cleared—in exactly forty-five days!

The big push was on. It was Operation Dismantle. Skilled technicians were needed to accomplish this task, but again God had His right men at the right place and time. Norman Blake had served a term with the FEBC as electronic engineer and was in America at the time on furlough. He offered, with the collaboration of Bob Reynolds, director of engineering, to do the dismantling.

The more delicate parts were removed first to insure against damage. A single transmitter tube can cost $500.00. The 100,000-watt GE transmitter was twice as powerful as any commercial broadcasting station licensed to operate in the United States. When used on one of the international shortwave frequencies, its voice could literally circle the earth with the speed of light. Although dead and silent as

Voice of America, it would live again to proclaim the words of Him who said, "Ye shall know the truth, and the truth shall make you free."

It was difficult to appreciate the size of the equipment. The main towers, of wood construction, were erected during World War II. A curtain-type antenna was suspended between each set of towers and was designed to concentrate the radio beam in a given direction with an effective radiated power of over *one million* watts. Heavy equipment was needed to remove the towers. The first contractor insisted the job was worth $17,000.00! Others were sought until they found a man who had suitable equipment and offered to do the job for $6,000.00.

When the original bidding had taken place, the Directors of FEBC actually sent two bids. The first was for $10,000.00 cash (which they didn't have); and on second thought, they decided to offer $30,500.00 to be paid over a period of five years. When the contract arrived, it asked for the $10,000.00 which they had offered in cash (and still didn't have) and the rest to be made in payments!

With the contract came a letter saying that they had received the $1,000.00 with the bid which showed their good faith. Now they were to look over the contract and send another thousand dollars (FEBC men had borrowed the first thousand to send with the bid!) and return the signed contract. They were told to start to dismantle the equipment, and after fifteen days to send another $3,000.00. Then, after another thirty days, they were to send another $5,000.00. That, together with the first thousand dollars, was to make up the $10,000.00 which the government considered to be the downpayment—but, that was *not* the way FEBC had meant it!

On the desk in the accounting department lay bills amounting to several thousand dollars. All Bowman and Roberts could do was thank the Lord for small favors, for the government didn't know they did not have ten thousand dollars in cash!

While they were sitting at the desk, reading all the fine print in the contract, Evelyn Esselstrom, FEBC's accountant, came to the door and said, "Here's something I think you ought to see."

Bowman answered without looking up. "Wait just a little. We are going over this contract right now."

"But I think you ought to see this now." Walking over to the desk she held in her hand a stock certificate which had come from St. Petersburg, Florida. A note said, "Sell this J.C. Penney Company stock and use it in the work you are doing." The Penney stock came in the same mail as the contract asking for $1,000.00.

Not knowing what the stock was worth, they put it in the hands of a broker. It had just gone up in price and they realized from it almost the exact amount they needed for the next payment.

Chapter Fifteen

RUSSIAN PRAYER MEETING

FIVE YEARS PRIOR TO THIS TIME, a group of Russian refugees
came out of Russian Turkestan, then over into Sinkiang,
China, and walked across China during the cold winter
months, finally arriving in Shanghai. They became wards
of the United Nations and were sent to the Philippines before proceeding to America.

Alex Chernov, one of the young men of the group, was
brought to Manila, where he had a leg amputated which
had been badly frozen while fleeing from the Communists
when crossing China. At this time he was invited to Christian Radio City where he gave his testimony over the radio
in the Russian language to be beamed back to his homeland.

Five years later, as Bowman and Roberts were in San
Francisco at the beginning of Operation Dismantle, they
felt the need to spend some time in prayer. Because most
prayer meetings are on Wednesday, and this was Thursday,
they had small hopes of sharing their burdens with some
group of Christians. In looking through a friend's church
directory they noticed one Russian church which had its
prayer service on Thursday. It was in an unfamiliar part of
San Francisco, and they wondered if they should try to
locate this church. Not knowing what to expect, but having
plenty of time, they set out to look for this small Russian
church.

About 8:00 P.M. they arrived in front of a large house
which had been converted into a church. The meeting was
in progress. Both Bowman and Roberts commented as they

got out of the car that they had never been on Russian Hill before and would be total strangers to this group. As they walked in, the pastor was speaking to his people. Then he looked back and briefly murmured something in Russian to those assembled, then said, "Well! Brother Bowman and Brother Roberts, come right up to the platform."

Bill Roberts thought as he walked up the aisle, "Who in the world is this man? I never saw him before in my life, and yet he seems to know us!"

The pastor said, "Brother Bowman, will you sing for us?" Bob walked over to the piano and sang a familiar church hymn.

Then he turned to Bill Roberts. "Now tell us what you are doing in San Francisco."

As he got up to speak, Bill Roberts thought to himself, "Well, I don't know who you are, but you asked for it." He told of how they wanted to increase their power so as to put a more powerful signal into the iron curtain countries. Then he related to them how God had provided the fifty-thousand-watt and one-hundred-thousand-watt transmitters there in San Francisco, and how they were in the very beginning stages of dismantling the equipment.

After Roberts was finished speaking, the pastor got up and spoke to the people in Russian. Both the guests wondered what was going on, but finally it became evident. Reaching down, the pastor placed an open Bible on the altar and invited the members to place their offering on the Bible. Bowman, watching an elderly couple at the rear, could hardly keep a straight face. The man leaned over and evidently asked his wife for some money. She obliged by handing him a one-dollar bill. He immediately shoved it back in her purse, reached over with his big hand, and grabbed a number of bills out of her billfold, then walked down the aisle with the others to place their offering on the Bible.

The pastor turned the meeting over to an elder and took Bowman and Roberts down to the basement where their eyes lit up when they saw some beautiful recording equipment.

Roberts asked, "Where did you get this elaborate equipment?"

Then the amazing story began to unfold.

Bob finally asked, "Let's see, what did you say your name was?" (They hadn't introduced themselves up to this point.)

The Russian pastor answered, "Demetrius."

"Not Paul Demetrius from Philadelphia?"

"Yes, I'm Paul Demetrius who lived in Philadelphia."

This pastor had been challenged by one of FEBC's missionaries who was on furlough some years before. Since then, Demetrius had been producing tapes in the Russian language for release over the Manila stations! What a coincidence. They knew each other but had never met!

Then Paul told how he had been called as a missionary to Russia but couldn't get in because of Communist activities. When he learned of the possibilities of radio, he devoted much of his time to the preparation of tapes.

It had been difficult to get recording material in Philadelphia from lack of suitable personnel. This same group of Russians, who had trekked across China in the winter, had formed a church in San Francisco upon their arrival and had given Russian Paul Demetrius a call to be their pastor. He finished with, "So, here I am."

Then it was revealed to Bowman and Roberts that some of the people still assembled upstairs were of the group that had come out of Russia via China and the Philippines to establish in America. Alex Chernov, who had lost a leg because of the trip, was a member of another Russian church.

Briefly, the pastor told of some of the bitter experiences these Christians had as they came across China. They

Two views of headhunters and their families hearing of Christ
for the first time.

Ilongot listeners hear the Gospel. Most of these have professed
Christ as Saviour. On extreme left is Dansal, the chief.

Typical village crowd listens to words of life via "PM" radio.

Many Negrito tribes are being evangelized by radio.

Family devotions around "God's box."

Customers of this Sari store are familiar with the Gospel message due to prominently displayed "PM."

Aerial view of KSBU antenna area (four towers), Okuma, Okinawa.

The 100,000-watt radio station KSBU, Okuma, Okinawa.

Diesel generator installed. Dick Caruthers, engineer, and his
Ryukyuan assistant.

Installation of diesel generator over which building was later
erected.

Listening to KSDX, Japanese language station, on "PM" radio.

Antennas pointing toward China mainland from 100,000-watt
station KSBU, Okuma, Okinawa.

buried their dead along the road. But now they had gained their freedom and could serve the Lord they loved without being molested.

Some of the older people in the church that evening were gravely concerned when Bowman and Roberts walked into the meeting. They, of course, did not know the leaders of FEBC, and took them to be secret agents (as the case would be in Russia) to check up on their producing tapes in the Russian language. Then it was explained to them who the strangers were.

* * * *

A heavy crane was brought in sections and assembled to a length of one hundred forty feet. It was hoped the towers could be lowered intact. But before they could be let down, the antenna curtain had to be dismantled and this called for skilled mechanics.

As a youth, Don Geary had fallen forty feet from a windmill tower. His back was broken: doctors said he would never walk again, but God delivered him from the life of an invalid to use him in His service.

As the antenna work progressed outside under Don's supervision, Norman Blake was busy inside the transmitter building, planning his work in such a way as to utilize all the man-hours possible. Skilled workmen came from every walk of life to give valuable assistance.

The removal of the shorter antenna poles was a comparatively simple operation. A small crane was used to lower the one-hundred-foot poles, but getting rigged for the job was the main task. There were four one-hundred-foot poles holding one of the main antenna curtains. Such poles in the Philippines would cost $3.00 a foot!

The antenna farm contained forty-five telephone poles which carried the transmission lines from the transmitter building to the different antennas. These were thirty feet long, and would be of great value overseas.

Some of the Russian refugees were the most faithful in helping dismantle the equipment. One of the men had night-shift work. He spent most of the day helping the FEBC men, taking just a few hours for sleep.

One cold foggy night, the others had gone home, but Bowman saw a man out where they had just lowered a tower. He wondered who it could be and decided to walk out to see. As he approached the spot, he saw Alex Chernov working hard removing some heavy turnbuckles. Dressed in a topcoat with the collar pulled up round his ears, Bowman spoke to Chernov. "Alex, it's too cold for you to be out here tonight."

Although the cold wind was blowing in off the bay, Alex never lifted his head nor lessened the speed of the wrench. In low tones he replied, "It is not as cold as China!"

Although the others had purpose in their being there, none had the impetus of the Russians, who realized some day this very equipment would be broadcasting the Gospel of Jesus Christ back to their homeland, Russia. Some of those giving assistance were business executives who would put on overalls and work along joyfully with the rest.

Fortunately, the location of the antenna setup was near the shipping dock, and not all of it had to be handled by truck. Shorter poles were snaked across the dock and bundled ready for shipment to the Philippines. A freighter came alongside the pier and loaded the poles and equipment aboard—a total of seventy-two and a half cubic tons. It consisted of seventy-five poles thirty feet long, four poles one hundred feet long, sixteen thousand board feet of structural lumber, and eight tons, or forty-one cases, of insulators and antenna hardware.

Lowering each of the main one-hundred-eighty-foot towers was a major operation. The idea was to lay them down intact. With a crane extended to the height of one hundred forty feet, the tower would be lifted off its base while a smaller crane would walk the bottom of the tower away from the base. Together they would lay it down on the ground.

As the engines were screaming, cables straining, the huge tower started to lift off its base—but, something happened! The tower snapped! A long bolt kept it from falling clear and caused the top section to swing like a club against the crane, crumpling it like a matchstick. The tower, cables, and crane fell in a twisted mass of wreckage around the cab. The crane operator—was he killed? As the cloud of dust settled, he crawled out of the cab, brushed off the dust, and exclaimed, "That was the roughest ride I have ever had!"

Clearing the wreckage, they found the cause of the accident—dry rot! And that was the tower Don Geary had just climbed. It wasn't possible to remove the towers as they had planned. The only thing to do was pull them over and salvage all the useable materials. The cables, insulators and other hardware were all precious and could be used in reconstruction overseas, but what a mess to be cleared away. A Russian refugee father and his son worked side by side, the father depending on the son for interpretation. Hawaiians, Chinese, Japanese worked hand in hand: it was like a United Nations. Missionary work is everybody's job.

Once a part of the skyline of San Francisco, the towers lay broken in splinters. They had been the Voice of Freedom around the world. But the heart of the voice were the transmitters and they were to be transported across the sea where they would live again. In a sense, that is what had happened to the Russian refugees that were helping. Elderly Pastor Bromanco, a leader of the refugees, who had walked across China, wore the marks of suffering in his face. Hundreds who started for freedom never made it. But of those who did, a new generation was born in the Land of the Free. Those who could, came to fight in the army of the Lord.

Forty-five days were not a long time in which to complete that task. Time was running out. Through the wise direction of the engineers and the consecrated labor of love by the volunteers, the work moved forward with incredible speed. What timbers could be salvaged were prepared for shipment. The rest were cleared from the property in order that the contract with the government might be fulfilled.

In the meantime, the remaining units were being removed from the transmitter building. Everyone worked feverishly hard, feeling the urgency of not only fulfilling the contract, but of getting the material ready for shipment at the earliest possible date. Everything connected with it was work, but there was a peculiar sense of the presence of Him who said, "I must work the works of him that sent me, while it is day: the night cometh, when no man can work."

It was a great day when the men looked out over the area and saw not a single tower standing. The last load of transmitter equipment disappeared out of sight on its way to the export packing company, where it was being prepared for overseas handling. A warehousing company offered to store the many enormous crates of precious equipment free of charge for six months.

*   *   *   *

Fred Freedmeyer volunteered to document Operation Dismantle with moving pictures. One day he called an old friend of his, who had been an important figure in international affairs, and said, "Why don't you come out with me today and watch the men work on the towers? The sunshine will do you lots of good."

A little later the two men drove into the antenna farm. The friend had spent several years in Moscow and noticed the Russian helpers at once. Being able to speak a limited amount of Russian, he started to converse with them. About this time, Alex Chernov drove up in his Oldsmobile and noticed several of the Russian helpers visiting with this onlooker. Upon entering the conversation, Alex mentioned how he had only two more payments on his car and how his family was growing. To have freedom and enjoy the things of this country were paramount in his conversation. The visitor turned to the engineers and said, "These men *know* what freedom is. This is the kind of story we should be getting behind the iron curtain."

All equipment was removed from the buildings and the outside area within the forty-five days! During that time the Lord had sent in $27,000.00 to cover the numerous bills that had piled up daily. As Bowman and Roberts sat at their desk to do some checking, they realized the needs had been met for the removal of the transmitter equipment and antenna, but over on the accountant's desk lay a stack of unpaid bills—the same amount that was owing when the project started—about several thousand dollars!

Strange as it may seem, people often rally to the support of some special project but give little thought to the regular operating expenses. With an operation such as FEBC's, just the cost of keeping the transmitters on the air is high. Monthly bills for power or for fuel oil for diesel generators, as the case may be, eat a big section from the monthly budget. Replacement parts for the equipment are not usually cheap. At one time surplus parts could be obtained, but they were expensive in the long run, and are no longer obtainable. Also, it should be remembered that FEBC does not charge the missionary to broadcast his programs over the stations. Therefore, monthly operating expenses must come through FEBC's home office.

Chapter Sixteen

UNLIMITED POWER

ONE ISSUE was holding up the shipment of the transmitter to Manila. Would the customs department charge 100 percent on the actual cost of the equipment to FEBC, or would the charge be based on the original value? There would be a considerable difference! (Both transmitters cost the U.S. government about three quarters of a million dollars!) FEBC was not prepared to pay the customs on the original value; the transmitter would be held up for months if the duty were charged on the actual cost.

Another problem which had shown up as serious some time before was diminishing somewhat. At the very time FEBC was trying to negotiate a fifty-thousand-watt transmitter to the Philippines, the Radio Control Board began to realize FEBC had been operating one transmitter far in excess of the legal amount. They were required immediately to reduce the power of a 10,000-watt transmitter to 3,000 watts. How sickening!

Since the government representative had returned from the Geneva conference and said, "Now it is the dog with the biggest bark that will be heard," it was understandable that more power should be considered. Even though the Philippines belonged to the International Telecommunications Union, which controls frequencies and power, it was understood each nation was sovereign unto itself. Therefore, if the Philippine government felt the need of boosting its power limits beyond its previous commitments, it had the right to do so without obligation to any other nation.

In doing so, however, an attempt was made not to interfere with other international stations.

Back in the days when John Broger applied for the first transmitter, the government was young: no one had much conception of the implications to follow. Out of the blue, John had asked for 10,000 watts of power, but when the application came back, remember, it had been penciled out and the words inserted, *unlimited power!* As soon as FEBC reminded them of this, the two 10,000-watt transmitters were put back into full operating capacity.

A number of factors were working together during those days. Friends in the Philippine government who believed FEBC operations were vital to peaceful conditions in Asia were working hard toward higher power transmitters for FEBC. Two giant voices were being stored in a west coast warehouse awaiting shipment. The visitor who had been invited to watch the dismantling of the towers in San Francisco—the one who had become interested in talking to the Russian helpers—had gone into action! And last but not least, Christians were praying that God would work.

A story which could take chapters evolved in one incredible miracle. Approval was given by the Philippine government for the 50,000-watt transmitter to be installed at Manila immediately! And through the influence of the visitor, arrangements were made for the equipment to be shipped to the Philippines *free of charge*. It would have cost FEBC over $12,000.00!

In the meantime, FEBC engineers were trying to procure a suitable location for the shortwave Overseas Service of Christian Radio City. In the selection of such a property, it was necessary to find an area big enough to accommodate the extensive antenna array associated with shortwave beaming techniques. The government offered public lands free of charge, but none was suitable. Weeks went by and not a single piece of property could be found. When time permitted, engineers literally scoured the countryside.

* * * *

During the months of negotiations and Operation Dismantle, things had by no means been at a standstill in Manila and in areas where FEBC broadcasts were beamed. An interesting mail survey had just been completed. Throughout the previous fifty months, 211,741 letters were received. Of these, 173,741 were written in regard to the Bible Correspondence Course (which now totaled more than 140,000 students). A total of 37,767 casual "tuner-inners" had written from 85 different countries of the world. Of course, that total did not include many who had written directly to the missionary who prepared the programs in other countries.

It is considered by many broadcasters in America that about one tenth of 1 percent of the radio audience will bother to write a letter to the radio station or program supplier. In Asia, it is doubtful if the percentage would be that high. However, using this basis, it means that the lives of almost thirty-eight million people had been reached in some manner by the ministry of Christian Radio City during the preceding four years!

Almost directly west of the Philippines lies the kingdom of Thailand with her nineteen million subjects, 89 percent Buddhist. Besides the Thai-speaking people, there is a large minority group that speaks Chinese. The signal from the FEBC transmitters in Manila covers this country effectively, bringing the only Gospel broadcasts in the Thai language.

Thailand missionaries have supplied FEBC with tape-recorded programs in the Thai language for a number of years. First among those to catch the vision was missionary-martyr Paul Johnson. Since his death others have risen up to carry on and to enlarge this ministry. A special broadcast studio was erected in his memory, and Missionary Webber has been assigned to the full-time job of preparing broadcast material. These programs aired twice daily from Manila have had rewarding results.

A Thailand missionary translated the following letters into English for the FEBC staff in Manila:

> This letter conveys to you the Christian greetings of Yao believers in the mountains of northern Thailand.
>
> Our leading believer, Brother Six, writes to tell you how happy he is to hear the Gospel going out over the air in so many languages. He has a radio in his home and listens quite faithfully to your broadcasts, especially the morning Chinese program. He understands Yunnanese Chinese, so enjoys listening to the various programs. He also understands Thai.
>
> He would like to convey the good wishes of the believers here and assure you that they are praying for you in your good work of spreading the Gospel.
>
> He would much appreciate the prayers of God's people in Manila for the church here. We trust that many more from among the Yao may soon believe the Saviour.
>
> Your brother in Christ,
> LAO LU

TO ALL THE BELOVED FRIENDS IN CHRIST:

Although we have not seen each other, we listen to your Gospel broadcast on the radio. We are all very happy about it.

I do not know what all your names are. And I hope that after receiving this letter you will pray for us, so that we and the family of Yao may have the power to labor for the Lord and be able to preach the Gospel to others. Here in our place, we have only very few believers. Those who believe in the devil are many, for they do not understand the light of God nor do they know that the Lord has died for their sins.

I hope you will pray to God to give us strength. It is already about three years since I received Christ as my own Saviour. Hope that you will pray for our Yao people here and also the church here.

Your brother,
PHAN KOI CHING

TO ALL THE MINISTERS IN CHRIST: We sent a letter before, but we do not know if you have received it or not. I listen to your broadcast and I am well pleased with your messages. I pray that when your broadcast is on the air you may be willing to pray for us, because it was already about three years that we believed on the Lord. We still don't have the strength to labor for the Lord, and also lack knowledge in the Word of God.

We live in one of the high mountains in Thailand. We are Yao tribe people. The Yao tribe people here in Thailand are many but are not Christians. Now we have more than twenty families that are working in the Lord's work.*

We were planting opium in order to earn our living before, but now we already have given up our old job, so please do pray for us that the Lord may give us grace and that He may open for us a new livelihood.* After receiving this letter, will you please write to us and also teach us?

PAN KWEI CHING (Christian headman)
PHANG GUAN ONG

A Buddhist priest from the famous temple of Dawn near Bangkok, Thailand, wrote:

I have listened to your program many times. I feel that the teachings of God are very profound because it

---

*Shortly after this letter was written, a missionary traveling in this area found *thirty* families serving the Lord.

*It was learned these people had turned to growing rice, which is far less lucrative.

makes my heart happy and right in a good way. I hope very much that you can enlighten me even more because I have known nothing about THIS WAY before.

From Yala, one of the southern provinces of Thailand, a border policeman wrote:

> I have believed in Christ for over a year now. I recently led two other policemen to Christ, and praise the Lord that they are already strong in Him. We now have services at my house every Sunday and more people are becoming interested. I have never been to Bible school, so I don't know very much to teach them. I would like to enroll in your Light and Life Correspondence Course so that I will be able to teach them better.

From a province in the northwest, a listener wrote:

> We are using the radio the missionary loaned us that receives only the Good News broadcast. We thank God for the opportunity to listen. When we hear the program in the morning we sing along with you and pray with you and listen to the reading of the Bible and the sermon.

At the same time, only several thousand miles farther to the west, a missionary writes a letter with a different sort of news!

> Yesterday we were notified that our contracts with Radio Ceylon will not be renewed, so when the present contract expires, it will all be over.* We are happy to hear that FEBC has purchased a 50,000-watt transmitter from the Voice of America. It appears that in the not-too-distant future FEBC will be the only possible means of reaching these areas with the Gospel message.

A situation parallel to this was happening in nearby India. An official committee of the Indian government was study-

---

*Production of Gospel programs aired over Radio Ceylon.

ing missionary activities in one of India's central states. The
report to the government from that committee was a blow to
evangelical Christianity. It urged that foreign missionaries
be withdrawn, charging that evangelism in India appeared
to be part of the uniform world policy to revive Christen-
dom for reestablishing Western supremacy. The committee
also recommended the right to propagate the Christian
faith be limited to Indian Christians, and that mission property be turned over to national groups or to Indian Christians.

A missionary who was traveling in the southern part of
India was conversing with a Danish missionary concerning
missionary conditions in general. The Dane did not know
the man to whom he was talking had anything to do with
radio. "During the past two years," he said, "we have had
more conversions than in the past twenty years. The people
have been coming out of the villages and looking up our
national workers. It has made it much easier for us."

The visiting missionary asked, "To what do you attribute
this?"

"We believe it is because so many people are listening to
the Gospel over the radio," he replied.

One of the programs beamed to India is the "Back to the
Bible Broadcast," produced by Theodore Epp in Lincoln,
Nebraska. For overseas releases they make special tapes
and mail them to Manila. On one particular broadcast, they
offered a Light and Life Bible Correspondence Course.
These international broadcasts do not use the Lincoln address but ask the listeners to write to their representatives
in the country to which the broadcast is beamed from Manila. However, some time ago the Lincoln address was used.

An eager listener in India wanted to enroll in the course,
so wrote to the Lincoln office. The staff in Lincoln wrote
him telling where he could get the course in India. His
letter to Nebraska and their reply to him had traveled about

twenty-four thousand miles. When he opened the letter, he was surprised to find he only had to go two miles down the road to pick up his course.

Back in the Philippines the PM's were continually humming with the Good News. In the southern part of Luzon a Presbyterian missionary had taken two PM's to his mission station to provide Gospel programs for some of the people in the nearby barrios. He planned to deliver them in a few days.

One day when he was gone, someone broke into the house, and among the things stolen were the two PM's. He reported it to the constabulary,* but nothing was heard about the PM's. Some time later, a constabulary officer was walking through a barrio some distance from where the missionary lived. He noticed a large group of people standing round one of the huts listening to a radio which was sitting on the windowsill. The policeman stood on the edge of the crowd for awhile and listened. Then suddenly he thought to himself, "Why, that looks like one of those radios that was reported stolen."

Making his way through the crowd, he reached up on the windowsill and took the radio down. Underneath he located the serial number and, by checking his notebook, found this to be one of the stolen PM's.

"Where did you get this radio?" was the stern question.

The owner answered, "Not long ago a fellow came along with two of them and offered one to me for fifty pesos. It was such a good bargain, I bought it."

When he had purchased the radio, he didn't know it had been pretuned to receive only the broadcasts from Christian Radio City, and was not a little perturbed! He tried to peddle it off on someone else, but was unable to. However since he was stuck with it, he decided he might as well use

*Philippine police force.

it. And the longer he had it, the more he became interested in what the PM had to say. Eventually he and his family were saved. They became so interested in the programs coming over the air, they placed the PM on the windowsill where the neighbors could come and listen.

After this man found out the radio had been stolen, he returned it to the missionary, who in turn reimbursed him the fifty pesos and told him how he could get another PM by applying to FEBC.

*　*　*　*

The Japanese releases were also showing good response. A missionary from Japan wrote FEBC, asking if they would mind if he came down to visit the station. A cordial welcome was extended to this man who forty years before had gone to Japan as an American businessman and an avowed atheist. He came in contact with the Gospel while there and was converted to Christ, later becoming a missionary.

Knowing the Japanese language well, he was invited to participate on one of the Japanese programs which would be beamed back to Japan. He gave his own testimony of his conversion from atheism to Christianity.

Some time later a letter was received in Christian Radio City from a Japanese telling that he had been listening that afternoon in his little home and heard the ex-atheist give his testimony. The Spirit of God moved upon his own atheistic heart, and he knelt on the floor and gave his heart to Christ.

A missionary writing from Japan told how she was one of those who thought radio couldn't be used of the Lord—that a personal contact was necessary—but admitted some things had happened in her area that had changed her mind.

One morning a man came to her door and, without the normal polite Oriental greeting, he bluntly said, "What can I do to be rid of the burden of sin?"

The missionary replied, "What has brought this to your attention?"

"I've been listening to a broadcast from the Philippines," was his humble reply, "and I have learned about it from there." She invited him into her home and had the joy of leading this seeking soul to Christ.

A little girl from Hiroshima wrote:*

> We have been listening to your broadcasts daily. As you know, Hiroshima experienced the first atom bomb. We learned one lesson from that bomb: Only love can save the peoples of the world. *Please* continue to send the message of the love of God to the people of my country.

A very wealthy businessman in Japan wrote to Manila telling the FEBC staff he had been moved by the messages he had been hearing. At the same time, a missionary wrote the station asking if he could help in any way with follow-up: "If you receive any letters from people in my area, I'd be happy to look them up and talk with them."

The letter was immediately forwarded to the missionary, who went to see the wealthy man. He was graciously received into the home, but at once learned of the desperate condition of the family. Because of sin, the home had been broken and suicide had been considered several times. The missionary could sense the trouble; it was evident this businessman wanted and needed salvation.

In dealing with the man, the missionary mentioned one touchy subject: "Probably God will require you to make up with your wife and take her back into the home."

*On a television program the pilot whose plane dropped the first atom bomb on Hiroshima was asked to describe what happened, and with quivering voice he replied: "We went in over the target. Looking down we saw a great sprawling city below. Then the bombardier began the count-down. Being dead on target, we heard 'Bombs away.' Turning rapidly we left the area as quickly as possible. Suddenly there was a blinding flash. We turned our plane and flew in over the target again. I looked down and cried, 'Oh, my God, what have we done!' Where a few moments before there had been a great city, now there was nothing but ruins and smoke ascending into the heavens."

At this the man replied, "If that is what it takes to be a Christian, I'll never be one!"

Feeling that he would be wasting time to further pursue the trouble, the missionary got up and left, saying as he went out the door, "Well, then, you will probably never be one."

Several weeks later the Japanese missionary received a letter saying, "You will never know how happy I am. Christ has changed not only my life but my home. My lovely wife and family are with me again and we all have become Christians. I am so appreciative of the broadcasts from Manila which sparked the desire, and for your frankness as you left my house. It was that last statement you made which caused me to face reality. Thank you so much!"

* * * *

But along with the blessings and encouragements which come in broadcasting the Gospel, there are problems and headaches. Engineers were almost frantic by this time. Not a single bit of property seemed to be available for the Overseas Service transmitters. Many considerations had to be made in choosing a location. It had to be far enough away from Christian Radio City so that the big transmitters would not interfere with the operation of the Philippine Service transmitters. It had to be far enough away from the metropolis of Manila to be satisfactory to the Radio Control Board, yet easily accessible to FEBC engineers. Geological features for ideal transmission must be considered.

Taking all that into consideration, the matter was placed before friends of FEBC in America who sought the Lord for His help. It is often the case that when people become burdened for some project, they start to react with monetary assistance. Concurrently, Dick Bronson, station director, was beginning to evaluate a piece of property ten miles north of Christian Radio City as money at the same time was being sent to the home office to purchase land.

With salt marshes and tidal river areas, engineers agreed

this land would be ideal for send-off conditions for radio waves coming from the 50,000-watt transmitter. Known as Bocaue, the site for the new transmitter building was very near Batia where the shelling occurred early in FEBC's history. Work was started immediately to build up a one-eighth-mile graded road, over the rice paddies, in from the highway. Three acres, the road, and lease cost $15,000.00. The antennas were to be built on twenty-five acres of rice paddies which were obtained on a long-term lease.

A four-thousand-square-foot building was begun as soon as the purchase was finalized. But, soon after the building started to take shape, no noise could be heard from the hammers. With the bank account depleted, work had to be terminated until more material could be purchased. Two things made it important that the job be finished at once: The transmitter would be arriving soon and it would be advantageous to put it directly into the new building. Second, the rainy season would soon be upon them. If the foundations for the antenna poles were not put in before the rains came, heavy trucks would not be able to get to the area. Work would be stopped until the rainy season was over and the ground hard once again. This would take many months!

Chapter Seventeen

END OF THE WESTERN
WORLD

CAREFULLY CONSIDERING THE SITUATION, the directors of
FEBC wondered if it were advisable to put both of the giant
transmitters in the Philippines. "We're surely putting all
our eggs in one basket!" asserted one. The 50,000-watt
transmitter had been shipped, but they thought it best to
hold the 100,000-watt unit in storage on the west coast until
they were sure where it should be placed.

Inspecting a map of Asia, the men spotted the island of
Formosa, but because of the fact that Free China, now oc-
cupying that island, was constantly in battle-preparedness,
it didn't seem feasible to locate there, even though a cordial
invitation had been extended to FEBC. Northeast of Formosa lay the small island of Okinawa. After considerable
discussion, it was agreed they spend the next days asking
the Lord if this was to be the place they were to locate the
mightiest voice of the FEBC stations. One thing was sure:
This transmitter was to be used to broadcast the Gospel of
peace to the enslaved millions in China.

✳ ✳ ✳ ✳

On April 1, 1945, the sky fell on Okinawa. It was Easter
Sunday. The combined forces of America's military might
began to pound hard on the door of the Japanese homeland.
Over 1,450 ships rendezvoused off the island's coral reefs.
Okinawa was the last main anchor in the Japanese defense
of her island empire. The United States and British forces
engaged here numbered over a half million men. New re-

cruits received their first baptism of fire. Veterans of other battles in the Pacific theater were moved up for this titanic assault.

First, resistance was deceptively light. Beachheads were secured with relative ease. The northern part of the island was occupied swiftly, but when our forces turned south toward the most heavily populated area, they met fanatical resistance, the ferocity of which had been hitherto unknown.

Okinawa was the last major ground battle of the war. It was also the most costly engagement of the Pacific. Casualties, including those killed, missing, or wounded in action, numbered 80,000. Over 12,000 American boys lost their lives. General Simon Buckner, commander of the Tenth Army, was killed by shell fragments on June 18, just a few days before the Japanese surrendered. Ernie Pyle, heroic news correspondent, also lost his life in this engagement. Okinawa saw action seldom witnessed in military history.

Thousands of GI's remember "Hacksaw Ridge" as the main defense line, where the Japanese made their fanatical stand. The enemy gun emplacements were so arranged that they covered every square foot of the American advance. Veteran Japanese troops moved in from Manchuria and fought side by side with Okinawans in a desperate effort to hold the line, because Okinawa was the last defense of Japan proper. They fought from the tombs and caves, hundreds of which dot the hillsides, but in the end they found no place to hide.

In the extreme south of the island stands Suicide Cliff. It rises sharply, overlooking the Philippine Sea. Shortly after 4:00 A.M. on June 23, 1945, Lieutenant General Mitsure Ushegema, commanding general of the 22nd Japanese Army, leaped to his death from the cliff. He was followed by his staff officers and hundreds of Japanese soldiers and civilians. What needless sacrifice they suffered because they believed a lie!

Finally enemy resistance was completely broken, but not until they had suffered over 120,000 casualties of whom an estimated 90,000 were killed. The thousands taken as prisoners found in the bitterness of defeat the sweetness of life possible only in surrender. Peace finally came to Okinawa.

The capital city of Naha lay in complete devastation. Skeletons from the past bore mute testimony of the bitter struggle. After eighty-two days the island was secure. America paid dearly for Okinawa. But the price for freedom is always high.

Okinawa, the largest island of the Ryukyuan chain, lies 350 miles off the coast of China, and is about halfway between Formosa and Kyushu, Japan. It is securely in the hands of the United States, and is a military protectorate, the status of which was fixed by treaty by the Department of Defense, with the Department of the Army as the executive agent. Authority is exercised by the High Commissioner, who supervises both the military and civil administrations.

Once called "the Rock," or "the Snake," it is fast becoming a "little America" in the Orient. The capital of Naha has been rebuilt into a thriving city of over fifty thousand inhabitants. East and West mingle on its streets. The American dollar is the medium of exchange. The people are friendly and comparatively prosperous, especially when judged by the standard of living in other countries of the Orient.

Prior to American occupation, the island could not boast of one single mile of paved road. Now, a network of paved roads crisscrosses the island, and construction is underway to completely circle the island with pavement.

It is a restless place—this dot in the vast Pacific—often swept by the dread force of mighty typhoons. Winds with gusts reaching nearly 200 miles per hour are not unknown. When a typhoon strikes, about all one can do is fasten everything as securely as possible and then wait out the storm, hoping that he as well as his belongings will still be there when it is past. Anyone who builds on Okinawa must not fail to reckon with the wind.

Restlessness is by no means confined to typhoons! Politically, the people are easily disturbed. Rabble-rousers have been active, endeavoring to whip up sentiment for reversion of the Ryukyus to Japan.

Communism, like the giant Goliath of old, challenges the world today and camps upon the doorstep of every nation. More than a political ideology, it is the devil's church in this world. It is a burning faith, proclaiming the coming triumph of man over adversity and evil, and man's eventual entrance, through science, into earthly paradise. Atheistic Communism worships the god of materialism. It has its prophets: Marx and Lenin; its hated evil: the capitalistic system; its purpose: world domination. But in spite of its successes, Communism also has its fears, one of which is that the Christ whom sinful men crucified, but who rose again, will allow His Word to be carried to hearts enslaved under the yoke of those who say, "There is no God."

The world stands, as it were, on "Suicide Cliff" today, and if it is not arrested in its mad rush, this generation will plunge into the abyss and perish eternally!

The religious life of the Okinawans shows a strong Buddhist influence, probably the result of the spread of that religion to Japan in the seventh century A.D., when the great Japanese Prince, Shotoku Taishi, was converted to Buddhism. Buddha's birthday is celebrated each year in tea ceremonies at Naminoure Shrine. However, no single religion can claim the worship of these island people. Never have the Okinawans known a Christian revival. They tend more toward the ancient belief of animism—that all objects possess souls, and that the spirits of the recently deceased remain active round the tomb. Consequently, they honor the spirits of the departed in annual ceremonies and spend more on construction of the tombs than on their homes.

For over two thousand years the emperors of Japan served as the high priests of the nation. At the close of World War II, Emperor Hirohito abdicated his throne as the "Son of Heaven" and said to the nation, "I am no longer God." General MacArthur cried for a thousand missionaries and millions of Bibles to flood Japan, in order that the vacuum left in the heart of the nation might be filled. His pleas met with pitifully little response. Now, the emperor has resumed his position as the high priest of the nation and again leads his ministers and people in worship at the Shinto shrine, where he prays for the souls of the departed and reports to his ancestors the state of the nation.

Every Shinto shrine is marked by the torii gate. It is a simple skeleton of the lintel and doorpost. Its origin probably dates back to the time of Moses, when God commanded Israel, just before they left Egypt, to sprinkle the blood on their doors. Passing beneath this sacred gate is supposed to purify the worshiper from the contamination of the outside world and prepare him to approach the temple and worship before the gods.

For over one hundred years Christianity has been preached in Japan (of which Okinawa has been a part), and yet, its combined missionary forces cannot boast half a million staunch adherents to the Christian faith. Yet, in the few short years since World War II, a new sect of Buddhism has gained over eight hundred million converts!

Not only religious zeal but extreme nationalism seeks to capture the patriotism of the people. It molds them into a fighting unit that will consider no act a crime if it seems to be committed in the interest of the state. Their lives are so dedicated to the cause in which they believe, that to slay or to be slain for their homeland is the highest honor attainable and a guarantee of future bliss!

One morning, Billy Reames, who was stationed in Japan at the time, and Bill Roberts walked into the office of the commander in chief of the Pacific operation, whose offices were in Tokyo. This officer, by virtue of this post, was also governor of the Ryukyus and was the logical one to contact first about admission to Okinawa.

However, just the day before, Billy Reames had been over to this office on another matter of business and had seen a display in the lobby showing a mimeographed booklet entitled *Militant Liberty* written by John Broger. On the front cover appeared a preface by the United States Secretary of Defense, with the following comment:

". . . At my invitation a special conference assembled in Washington in June, 1955, to discuss the optimum aspects of a Free World ideology in connection with a concept called MILITANT LIBERTY—a thesis prepared by Mr. John C. Broger, President of the Far East Broadcasting Company, now serving as consultant in the Office of the Joint Chiefs of Staff . . ."

On the display were draped American flags and a letter by the officer in charge saying that this should be implemented throughout his command in the Pacific as a training program for military personnel.

Needless to say, it wasn't necessary to give a lengthy introduction of FEBC, as the men were thoroughly acquainted with the work being carried on from Manila. After showing some photos of the 100,000-watt transmitter, the concept of the program was presented. Since the giant voice was to be used in the Overseas Service for China, the purpose was to present the moral and spiritual principles which constitute the foundation of freedom and democracy, and to lay a foundation of understanding. It was suggested by the officer to go to Okinawa and see the High Commissioner.

When Bill Roberts arrived in Okinawa, he found the man in charge engrossed in his own problems. It didn't appear there were any objections to establishing the 100,000-watt transmitter there, but what was bothering the High Commissioner was the fact that just two weeks before, the capital city of Naha had elected a Communist mayor! Okinawans had been provided schools, a university, hospitals, clinics, and many other benefits by a democratic system; yet when they were given the freedom of election, they used the liberty to *elect a Communist mayor!*

The High Commissioner thrust the question at Roberts: "What can we do about this problem? If we cannot reach the minds of these people with some kind of understanding of the responsibility that goes along with their liberties, then we have missed our goal!"

At this, Roberts suggested the possibility of setting up a small transmitter to broadcast to the Okinawans, and the idea was affirmed. This would do the island a great service. It was also agreed that it would be in the interest of the free world if FEBC were permitted to build a powerful radio station on Okinawa, from which the message of hope could be beamed to the enslaved peoples of China—only 350 miles away.

Twelve acres of land were leased out for the first station— the low power for Okinawan service. One of the finest hospitals in the Orient, a multimillion-dollar structure, had just been dedicated. It replaced the old quonsets of Mercy Hospital which served the military personnel and native population for ten years. Two of these quonsets were secured for temporary studios. Within nine months after the initial contacts were made on the island, FEBC's radio station KSAB went on the air bilingually, reaching the English-speaking population as well as the Okinawans who speak Japanese.

Among the guests visiting the station were missionaries working on the island, military personnel interested in such a project, and two Polish refugees who were crew members on a ship. When their captain changed orders to head for Shanghai, they refused to sail for fear of being recaptured by the Communists. They said they would jump into the sea rather than take the chance of being forced to return behind the iron curtain.

Frank Ineson, who had spent two years with General Mac-Arthur's staff in Japan, was director of the station. Arthur Austin was in charge of design and construction, while Bob Kellum kept things lit up as chief engineer. Local technicians and office help rounded out the staff.

With the news that a powerful station could be built on Okinawa, Operation Transportation was begun. From the docks of San Francisco, one hundred tons of precious radio equipment were loaded aboard the "Tarheel Mariner," bound for Okinawa. Judging from the various sizes of the crates and the nondescript appearance of some of the gear, such as guy wires, it was difficult to realize the value of the component parts. The power transformer grossed in at nearly eight tons as it was hoisted on the deck. Thousands of pieces, large and small, were crated in heavy overseas packing and carefully marked.* The port authorities in Naha agreed to store the 100,000-watt transmitter, when it arrived from San Francisco, until its permanent home could be prepared. And, again, as had been done on the 50,000-watt unit sent to Manila, free transportation was provided!

Jim Copal, who had first spotted the giants on the San Francisco skyline, and who had been working as engineer in Manila, went up to Okinawa to help Bill Roberts survey the island for a suitable site for the large station.

About fifty miles north of Naha is Okuma, a small neck of land surrounded on three sides by the East China Sea. It is

---

*An explanation should be given about the words "carefully marked." It is more accurate to say that since it was first believed both transmitters were to go to Manila, parts were not separated as they should have been. Thus, a few parts of the 50,000-watt unit arrived in Okinawa, and some parts for the 100,000-watt unit arrived in Manila.

fastened to the mainland by a low strip of land not more than ten feet above sea level. The road to Okuma winds along a very rugged coastline. Surf rolls in over coral reefs, transforming this coastline into pictures only the Divine Artist could paint. But when typhoons lash the sea, it takes great bites out of the coastline. Often work crews are busy repairing the road which runs along the water's edge. In the Orient, women share the common labor with men. They know little about the drudgery of housework but talk with authority about gravel and cement!

Buses on their regular schedule pass along beautiful rice fields, wayside shrines, and villages. They are not taken as much for granted as if they had always been there. The last twenty-mile stretch of road is unpaved and narrow, besides having other hazards. There is a small tunnel that would hinder the hauling of high loads, and just beyond this is a bridge which was damaged during the war and has never been completely rebuilt. It was over this road Roberts and Copal watched heavy military vehicles travel and wondered how they could ever transport one hundred tons of bulky radio equipment. It didn't take long before they were convinced it would have to be brought in by sea.

Okuma was not only the best spot for the transmitter but the only place it could be allowed. On the southern end of the island were literally dozens of important transmitters and receiving stations maintained by the military. The signals from high-power transmitters would interfere with receiving stations. Therefore, the Voice of America megawatt transmitter and FEBC's 100,000-watt station would have to be isolated on the northern part of the island.

An officer's rest center was located at Okuma, where they could bring their families on vacation. Next to the center, a golf course had been planned. After scouring the area for the best site, a request was made for outleasing the plot next to the center. "But that is the place we have planned to put the golf course!" was the immediate reply. "See if you can find some other place."

More time was consumed looking, but there was no place as suitable as that area. In answer to the next request, this reply came: "Yes, you may lease that area. We will put the golf course some other place." Thirteen acres of land were available for the site of the giant transmitter.

Other problems were developing. As FEBC engineers sought for a frequency, they found it to be a strangely different setup than in other countries. Okinawa, under military protectorship, did not have a radio control board such as other countries had. Matters like this came under the Far East Command of the U.S. Forces in Tokyo. And when a request was put in for a frequency for the 100,000-watt transmitter, the reply came back: "Please be advised that 3,000 watts of power is maximum for the island of Okinawa." THREE THOUSAND WATTS! And there on the island, in storage, FEBC had a transmitter that would make a 3,000-watt job look like a midget!

As soon as this reply was made known to the local authorities, a letter was forwarded to the office in Tokyo: "The General is not pleased with your report . . ." Not long after, a letter came from Tokyo stating that 100,000 watts of power would be unreasonable to consider since it would interfere with Japan. However, if they could submit an engineer's report showing some way to shield Japan, it would be considered.

At once Roberts and Copal sent the necessary information to an engineering firm in San Francisco, who shortly after returned drawings of a four-tower antenna array which would definitely block out any interference with Japan. The plans were immediately forwarded to the High Command Office in Tokyo with a request for 850 kilocycles—medium wave. Without delay, an answer came back saying, "We did not understand you were talking about medium wave.

We thought you were requesting a frequency for shortwave."
This cheerful note was added: "But after carefully looking
over the plans, it appears your engineering firm has given
sufficient proof that you can keep Japan clear from any interference."

From Jim Copal's survey of the land at Okuma, it appeared they would be running into serious trouble, since
there were two hills on the property. This would interfere
greatly with the four-tower antenna array. There was nothing to do but move those hills away. But what about the
cost? The advice of an army engineer was sought. He estimated the job would cost $35,000.00. But on second thought,
he had an idea! "Why not see the marines here on the island!
They often have large training projects where they teach
marines to use heavy earth-moving equipment. You know,
they might just be willing to train some young leathernecks
on a project like this."

Bill Roberts went immediately to see the general. He explained thoroughly the purpose for this radio station—to
reach China with the message of Christianity. Never flinch-
ing an eye nor showing the slightest response, the general
sat at his desk looking at some papers. Roberts added, "But,
General, we have a problem. There are two hills on this
antenna farm and I wonder if we could get your cooperation
in pulling them down?"

At this question the general stood up, walked around his
desk, and stared Bill Roberts in the eyes. He replied, "Sir!
This is not a matter of cooperation. This is a matter of duty.
We can boast ourselves of atomic power to grind nations to
dust; but if we do not reach their hearts and minds, we will
change nothing but the map! Sir! We not only can, but we
shall pull those hills down! If you intend to hit the beaches
of China with the message of freedom and democracy, we
may not have to land our men on them later!"

In a few days, marines were rolling into Okuma as if to

establish an important beachhead! The Bible speaks of faith to move mountains, but sometimes faith and works are a necessary combination to do the job. Literally, the two hills—one 60 feet and the other 40 feet high—were removed and the twelve hundred cubic yards of dirt used to fill in the valley. The building site had to be raised six feet. A quarter-of-a-mile road was built into the property. After the site was finished, the general turned to Bill Roberts and asked, "Now, is there anything else we can do to help?"

Time goes fast. Though it didn't seem like it, a year had gone by since the first contacts were made for establishing the work of FEBC on the island of Okinawa. And now, everything was in readiness to start construction of the transmitter building.

Chapter Eighteen

UNUSUAL PROVISIONS

DURING THE YEAR just expired, things had moved along so well in Okinawa; but the same could not be said for the transmitter project in Bocaue. Money was slow coming in to complete the transmitter building. But more disturbing, the 50,000-watt components were sitting outside in the weather beside the buildings at Christian Radio City, although they were covered to protect them from the downpours of rain. Bob Reynolds was getting grayer by the month, wondering what was happening inside the big crates.

Another international broadcasting station had shipped a 50,000-watt transmitter to the Philippines sometime before and, because of some unavoidable circumstances, they too had to store their unit outside. At the end of the period they found the equipment in bad shape and spent about $10,000.00 to repair and replace parts corroded beyond use. What was happening to FEBC's transmitter out in the weather? With the rainy season very close, they pushed ahead as fast as the bank account would permit.

Occasionally someone in the Orient would come up with the idea that the Far East Broadcasting Company was nothing but a United States Government front. "No one could be so dedicated as to give their lives to the cause of spreading the Gospel. They surely are deceptive!" Some declared, "This must be a forerunner for the military. The missionaries come first, soften the people with love, then the military comes next and takes over the country after the people

166

have been taught to love their neighbors! FEBC must be a government front!"

If such characters could have attended some of the prayer meetings where missionaries and leaders were asking God to supply the means to finish some of the pending projects, they wouldn't have wondered about its being associated with the government. The only connection, of course, is that FEBC leaders and staff believe in the principles on which America was founded: freedom, liberty, and justice for all! Our country is great because our forefathers honored God.

Back in the home office there was a desperate need for $20,000.00. With two major projects going on—one in Okinawa and the other in Manila—supporters forgot that a monthly budget had to be met. By now, FEBC had changed their original policy concerning workers' support. At first, FEBC paid all the allowances. Later, each missionary was asked to raise his own support before going to the field. Yet, there were still dozens of drains on the general income. Power bills and maintenance costs were getting higher as they expanded their programs. The monthly budget was $24,000.00 for the entire work, excluding money for different projects.

Seven years before, a wealthy Christian businessman in Shanghai, China, was able to get a part of his savings out of China just before the Communists took over the country. John Broger had met the man and learned of his heavy burden to build Christian radio stations in China. One small station was constructed in Shanghai but operated only a short time after the Communists arrived. This Christian was dragged into court several times because of his testimony and desire to spread the Gospel. Since he had been very much weakened by a prolonged illness, the authorities told his wife she could nurse him until he appeared before the court again. He never entered the courtroom but passed into the presence of his Saviour. Just before he died, he heard a Christmas program in Chinese coming from Manila—songs of the church he loved so much, and a message from God's Word. Right away, he sent a coded message to his son living in the United States. It said something to this effect: "Draw all my money out of the bank in Chicago and send it to the Far East Broadcasting Company." Shortly, a letter from the son said, "My father has requested me to draw the remainder of his savings out of a Chicago bank and send it to you to be used in spreading the Gospel by radio. In a few days I shall be sending you a check for $20,000.00." God's ways of working are indeed mysterious.*

With this large gift, the monthly allotment to Manila was full for the first time in months. Work on the transmitter building progressed rapidly. It would soon be ready for the installation of the big transmitter.

One grave concern was facing the directors and engineers of FEBC. None of their men had ever worked on anything bigger than 10,000 watts of power, and there is a considerable difference between that and 50,000 watts!

In Big Rapids, Michigan, a Christian by the name of Clyde Hull was awakened from his sleep. The Lord seemed to be speaking to him about contacting FEBC in Whittier, California and offering his services. Mr. Hull had been employed by Voice of America and had put their one million-watt transmitter on the air in the Philippines, and had helped set up 50,000- and 100,000-watt transmitters in North Africa. He did not know that FEBC had purchased the big giants. Strangely enough, he was led to offer his services to FEBC.

It wasn't long before Clyde Hull was standing beside the crates in Manila as they started to rip off the first boards.

*This story is being told for the first time. Just recently the aged wife made her escape from Communist China and will be living in America with her son the rest of her life. She reports KSBU is heard loud and clear in Shanghai.

God had met the need for a man capable of assembling equipment of this size. And to the astonishment (and thanksgiving) of all standing there, every piece which was uncrated appeared to be in excellent condition.

Work moved along steadily on the transmitter during the latter part of the dry season. Norman Blake, Mr. Hull, and a Filipino helper were kept busy every day cleaning, polishing, fitting, checking, and sorting. The gutters in the concrete floor were collecting their allotment of wires, and over them various parts of the unit were taking shape.

But outside the building a different picture could be seen! Byrd Brunemeier and Jack Lentz and a big crew of Filipinos were having a frantic race with the weather. The antenna poles had to be set before the rains came—and it would commence to rain any day! Every day the clouds were heavier and darker. Occasionally a few sprinkles would act like a shot of adrenalin to a dying man. There were still five 100-foot poles to go up, and each pole stood on a concrete pedestal with its guy wires attached to huge concrete "dead men" buried in the ground.

Bob Reynolds, director of engineering, wrote:

"Wednesday was the day we had engaged the crane to set the five 100-foot poles for the antenna farm. Tuesday night it started to rain. By Wednesday morning the rice paddies were nice and slippery on top. The rig got stuck twice getting out to the site of the first pole. There were intermittent showers during the five hours the poles were set. As they were setting the last pole, the sky to the east became very dark and it was evident we were in for a severe storm. As soon as the last pole was set, the crane started out of the rice paddy for safety on dry ground. And just as it pulled up on the filled roadway by the transmitter building, the rain really started coming down. As I drove the ten miles back to Christian Radio City, the water was up over the road, so you can imagine what the rice paddies were like by then. If we hadn't been able to get the poles in just when we did, we wouldn't have had the antennas up until next year!"

Inside the transmitter building, components were being placed in their proper cabinets. Expectancy was building up fast as the engineers realized it wouldn't be too long before the power switch could be thrown and this giant would sing with power.

Days of final checking and rechecking followed. Circuits were checked individually. There was no on-the-air deadline such as DZAS had to make when it first hit the air waves! More time than can be imagined was taken to be sure everything was checked out perfectly.

Then the mistake was found—a blunder of the ages. (Fences and gates are installed round the high-power components so that a person will not walk into some of these units and be electrocuted. If a gate is opened while the transmitter is on, it will automatically shut off.) One of the holes in the concrete floor, where a gate lock was to fit, was off two inches! What a blunder! A man quickly chiseled a new hole while the rest of the crew ruefully laughed it down.

Nearly 150,000 to 200,000 watts of power are consumed by a 50,000-watt transmitter. The day the master switch was thrown, the heavy-duty electric meter installed by the power company about went crazy. One of the Filipino boys was heard saying, "Waoo! I'd hate to pay that power bill!"

The giant operated normally from the very start, which was a colossal achievement. For the first few days it kicked off because of overloads. The difficulty was found each time and corrected. Then came the time for it to be put into service. This occurred on the tenth anniversary of radio station DZAS. The following official message was sent from the President of the Philippines:

It is with great pleasure that I greet the Far East
Broadcasting Company—its management, staff, and millions of listeners—on the occasion of the tenth anniversary of Radio Station DZAS.

I am most gratified to know that this radio station—
aside from being an instrument in helping form public
opinion and in enabling the masses to appreciate the
higher things in life—is proving itself to be a force in
strengthening Freedom and Democracy in Asia. This,
I understand, it is trying to accomplish through its missionary work of dedicating itself to the service of God
and mankind. The DZAS, indeed, is a station with a
high mission.

I wish this station greater success.

CARLOS P. GARCIA
President of the Philippines

What had taken place during a decade of broadcasting
the Gospel in the Orient? Staff members were challenged
as they searched the files and came up with the following
information:

1948   DZAS   680 kc—1,000 watts on the air. Building continues on missionary housing and studios.

1949   DZH6   6.030 mc—First "Call of the Orient" shortwave
station on the air. Languages and dialects of Far
East for overseas release are added to schedule.

1950   DZH7   9.730 mc—Second shortwave station added.
Portable missionary construction is started. First PM
travels to island of Panay. 300-foot antenna erected
by FEBC staff and Filipinos.

1951   DZH8   11.885 mc
       DZB2   3.345 mc
       DZH9   15.300 mc—Three more international short-
wave stations added. Split service employed, using

one group of transmitters for overseas, another for Philippine coverage simultaneously. 36 languages and dialects of the Far East employed.

1952   DZI6   17.805 mc—Sixth shortwave station added.

1953   Project to purchase two 10,000-watt Collins transmitters.

1954   DZFE   1030 kc—Manila's "Fine Music" station on the air. First 10,000-watt Collins transmitter on the air.

1955   Second Collins transmitter on the air.

1956   Two giant transmitters, 50,000 watts, purchased and dismantled in San Francisco for shipment to Far East.

DZI8   21.515 mc—Seventh Call of the Orient shortwave transmitter added.

1957   KSAB   1020 kc—On the air on Okinawa for Ryukyuan coverage. 100,000-watt transmitter shipped to Okinawa. 50,000-watt transmitter shipped to Philippines. Bible School of the Air announces "quarter of a millionth student" enrolled. First stereophonic broadcast made in the Orient.

1958   FEBC celebrates its tenth year of broadcasting the Gospel to the Orient and rejoices in God's goodness. Nine stations on the air at Manila, broadcasting 20 hours daily in 36 languages and dialects. Eleven separate antenna systems. Response letters from 85 countries. Portable Missionary army increased to over 900. Okinawa coverage station on the air. Recording facilities in Hong Kong. 76 staff members in the Philippines. 20 staff members on Okinawa. 3 staff members in Formosa. 2 staff members in Hong Kong. 13 on the home office staff in Whittier, California.

One of the Filipino boys who had become an operator at the Bacaue transmitter site was none other than Feliciano Cristobal, the first convert of Batia. From the transmitter building at Bacaue, Batia could be easily seen across the rice paddies!

Chapter Nineteen

FIRE! FIRE!

READY-MIXED CONCRETE was not available at the western end of the world. Footings for the transmitter buildings were laid five and one half feet below the level of the ground. Cement had to be mixed by hand. Reinforcing steel was welded together. The building, forty by sixty feet, would house just the transmitter.

John Lin, a Chinese from Formosa, was foreman of a Nike installation not far away, and donated many after-working hours as structural engineer. The building had to be well planned. Not only plumbing, but heavy conduit as well had to be laid under the floor to accommodate the intricate wiring of the transmitter.

Missionary Bill Quisenberry volunteered to lay the cement blocks. Talk about a job! Three thousand six hundred forty-six blocks were lifted over the protruding ends of the reinforcing rods and set in place. Wherever two rods crossed, they had to be welded together to completely ground the building from electricity in the air. A total of 14,400 feet of reinforcing steel was used. It's no wonder Quisenberry wrote on one block near the top *"Ebenezer,"* as he could say without any doubt, "Hitherto hath the Lord helped us."

The roof as well as the walls had to be made of concrete, in order that it might be typhoonproof. To insure against cracks, the entire roof was poured at one time. The largest available mixer at the end of the western world was finally obtained, and it looked pitifully small for the job! A hoist lifted the cement thirteen feet to the top of the roof and a faithful crew of Ryukyuans kept it flowing. The twenty-

four-hundred-square-foot floor space was finished with a
dustproof topping. Within three months to the day from
the time it was started, it was completed to the extent that
the transmitter could be moved in. Men from the army, air
force, marines, navy, seabees, Voice of America—Chinese,
Japanese, Okinawans, and Americans, both civilians and
service personnel—joyfully and voluntarily labored on the
project. Even the weather cooperated! The work was accomplished during typhoon season, but not a single one
struck the island throughout the period of construction.

Back in Naha, very early one morning, one hundred tons
of precious radio equipment were loaded aboard two utility
landing craft which set out in the gray dawn for Okuma,
fifty miles north. One carried a bulldozer, heavy trucks, and
a mobile crane capable of lifting the eight-ton power transformer!

Since there was no pier at Okuma, the ships had to reach
their destination by noon to hit the beach at high tide. One
ship started for shore a little early and rammed the coral
reefs. The other ship waited and came in without incident.
The bulldozer rolled off first so as to push sand up to the
ramp of the ship. The heavy crane swung the radio equipment onto the trucks and, with the help of the bulldozer,
hauled it ashore.

About one half mile away, another crane was ready to
unload the truck at the door of the transmitter building. The
entire operation was accomplished without injury to a single
workman or damage to a piece of equipment. Once inside,
the components were removed from their shipping cases
where they had been safely kept for many months.

There was no letup of expense with such massive projects.
The estimated cost of changing the shortwave transmitter
over to medium wave (or the standard broadcast band) was
$8,000.00! Four 260-foot steel antenna towers were to be
erected soon. The cost of the steel towers alone was

$20,000.00, which the Lord met. Intricate phasing equipment for tuning the directional antenna was still to be purchased at a cost of $13,000.00.

*   *   *   *

Reception reports from distant parts of the world rang with a note of challenge as the 50,000-watt transmitter spoke forth from Manila:

Pakistan: "Reception perfect even on an old battery radio."

India: "It is pleasant to hear . . . loud and clear."

Africa: "Reception perfect at all times."

Laos: "Signal strong and clear."

Ethiopia: "What a thrill! We are hearing you in our mission station here in Ethiopia. Volume is excellent!"

Assam: "I wish to inform you that I tune in to your program as I can. Reception is excellent. I live in a place which is 20 miles away from the nearest church, but I am happy I am not deprived of God's message even here."

Assam: "The broadcast has been a source of blessing to my soul and has, thank God, changed my life completely. I would rather miss my food than miss the daily messages from your broadcast."

*   *   *   *

One year later, the 100,000-watt transmitter was nearing completion. However, it would remain a cold inanimate object until electrical current could surge through its arterial system. Okuma—at the end of the western world—had no power lines nearby! To operate a 100,000-watt transmitter at peak capacity requires 300,000 watts of power. Not a single person in the entire FEBC staff knew about diesel generators that large.

Richard Bronson, now back in the home office, had a friend who had been with the Cummins Diesel Company for over thirty years. He had started working with diesels in logging camps in the Pacific Northwest and had worked with heavy equipment all his life. This friend, Bronson said, was a Christian, retired, and living in Long Beach. A phone call from the Whittier office queried Dick Caruthers as to what he was doing. "Oh, just sitting around listening to the band concerts during the day and playing shuffleboard in the evenings and waiting for a heart attack so I can go to be with the Lord," was the answer!

At 67 years of age, the Lord tapped him on the shoulder and said, "I need you!" Starting in all over again, he and his white-haired wife volunteered to go as missionaries to Okinawa! But first, a generator-engine unit had to be found. Prices ranged from $40,000.00 to $50,000.00. Then, someone heard of a surplus unit in Washington state for $16,000.00. It was a 300,000-watt unit and never used except as a stand-by: only a few hours were recorded on the hour meter.

Dick Caruthers was given the total responsibility of purchasing, crating, and shipping the thirty-two-ton generator to Okinawa. Believing it was better to ship it as one complete unit, he had to engineer a strong steel base to keep it in perfect alignment en route. Instructions were given him to take every wrench, bolt, and nut that he would need, plus replacement parts, as there would be no place where he could turn for service within thousands of miles!

After taking three months in transit, the generator arrived in Okuma. A landing craft hauled it to the transmitter site from Naha, just as the other equipment had been brought in, and a fifty-ton crane carried it over and set it right on its base which had been prepared some weeks before.

Ray Meeks, a Christian contractor from the United States, volunteered to build the power-plant building after the diesel was installed on its base. It couldn't be built first, since they had no way to get the huge unit inside. Ray had built the Overseas Service transmitter building in Manila several years before and was happy to oblige again. But, lo and behold, as he was ready to leave, he took a valuable piece of FEBC property—Lois Viet, a second-term missionary and a worker in the program department of KSAB in Naha.

During the time other major projects took the attention of most of the staff, a second station, KSDX, was added to the service in Okinawa. This would make possible a complete English block for KSAB, and the new station would be devoted entirely to Japanese programming for the 850,000 Okinawans.

* * * *

After fourteen years of fellowship in the ministry of FEBC, it was with regret that the resignation of John C. Broger was accepted. In May, 1954, Admiral Radford, then Chairman of the Joint Chiefs of Staff, asked Broger to serve as a consultant for a period of forty days. That period turned into six years, the last four of which he was Deputy Director of the Office of Armed Forces Information and Education.

At the time of Broger's resignation, Robert Bowman became president of the Far East Broadcasting Company, William Roberts was made vice-president and secretary, and Andrew Nelli was added to the three-man Board of Directors as treasurer.

* * * *

Immediately following a cable telling of the emergency, an airmail letter was sent to the home office by Janie Reames, wife of the director of KSAB and KSDX. It read:

"Last Wednesday morning at 1:00 A.M., we were awakened by the telephone ringing, and the message we heard just dropped the bottom out of our world. Our beautiful studios and offices were going up in flames! Billy was dressed and gone in a few minutes. After he was gone, I dropped to my knees and sought help and comfort and guidance from the Lord.

"At 2:30 A.M. Billy called me to say the studios and controls and all the electronic equipment were destroyed or badly damaged. The fire started in the KSDX control room evidently from a short in the wiring. Most of the missionary men of our staff were there, frantically trying to save what they could. First thought was to save hundreds of dollars worth of tapes and recordings which were not replaceable. Praise God, they were able to save most of them, though many were damaged by smoke and heat.

"Billy asked me to get coffee and toast ready for the men. He came and got me, and we were at the station the rest of the night and of course all the next day. What a pitiful sight! We went in with flashlights to view the ruins. Some of our men cried like little children to see the work of more than two years burned to a crisp. It would have broken your heart to see those men, blackened with smoke and wet with sweat, with tears running down their cheeks. Not a one of them was discouraged!

"At 2:00 A.M., while the firemen were still fighting the remaining areas of smoldering fire, the men had a prayer meeting in Billy's office and got up and started to rebuild. Immediately, they began to put together another control—pulling out burned pieces of equipment, hunting spare parts from other buildings, patching up a control that would at least allow them to get on the air with something by regular sign-on time in the morning. I have never seen such a demonstration of great faith and determination and love for God.

"We all worked, searching out stuff that could be cleaned up, salvaged, and used in the temporary setup. Try to picture us working through the dark of the night in a burned-out building, wading through water left by the firemen, and picking things up in our arms that were charred and burned! We were a sight to behold. Black, dirty, hot, and tired—but praising the Lord! The thought came to me through the night, 'He will give beauty for ashes.'

"At 6:25 A.M., *just twenty-five minutes later than our usual sign-on time,* we were on the air with a testimony that has moved listeners throughout Okinawa and has glorified our Saviour.

"That first day, we were on the air the entire day with an English announcer and a Japanese announcer sitting side by side at a scorched microphone in front of a pitiful-looking control, telling listeners on both our stations what had happened and how we believed Romans 8:28. Our transmitters were not hurt and so with the one control we could broadcast simultaneously over both stations.

"By daylight there were many of our friends on hand to help, and the Ryukyuan staff arrived for their regular workday. There were many tears shed as each one came and saw the destruction, but the beautiful thing was to see them pitch in immediately and to hear them say, 'We will build a new station.'

"At nine o'clock in the morning the entire staff and friends met in the ruins of the KSDX program office for prayer. What a precious time of fellowship in suffering with the Lord and with one another. Some have said the fire was worth it—to inspire such a meeting. After prayer, the staff scattered in all directions and worked like beavers throughout the day.

"Through this tragedy we have seen God work in a manner which we have never seen before. We have found we have friends we never dreamed of. Many have sent or brought in offerings. Gifts of equipment, volunteer labor, well-wishes, assurances of prayer, and offers of help in many ways.

"The Armed Forces Radio has loaned us, for an indefinite period, a complete mobile unit equipped with studio controls, console, turntable and tape recorders. This is what enabled us to get the second station on the air the second day. It has rejoiced our hearts to see how God works. We believe through it all we will have a better station than ever before."

Chapter Twenty

MIGHTY VOICE TO CHINA

ON THE ISLAND OUTPOST of democracy, Okinawa, KSBU went on the air, proclaiming the Gospel, on the standard broadcast band. The four-tower directional antenna system increased its 100,000-watt power to an estimated effective radiation of over one million watts, centered on Shanghai, China. Fanning out north of Peking and south of Canton, the signal penetrates several thousand miles inland. This means the Chinese who are under the heel of Communism can receive the signal on their millions of standard-broadcast-band radios. There were an estimated 4,500,000 receivers in China in 1961, and there is evidence that China is producing 100,000 new radios each year.

This thirteenth and largest transmitter of the Far East Broadcasting Company stations took the prayers, gifts, and labors of a great number of consecrated men and women. It was an undertaking immense in its scope, impossible in the natural, and foolish to those without faith.

The free world has conceded the loss of the entire nation of China. The Christian world has been forced to acknowledge the formidable barriers to the Gospel that have arisen around China's seven hundred million souls. No missionary has entered China since the Communists took over. Yet, Christ has not lost the battle. He will not make concession to the enemy grasp on those souls. There are many in China He died to save. His voice must go forth to save them!

Behind the scenes of this mighty voice works an unseen group of young Christian Chinese. Without them, KSBU's gigantic power would be of no value. In a well-equipped

studio on the eighth floor of a Hong Kong office building,
Riley Kaufman and his Chinese staff labor day after day to
produce the very best in programs for listeners behind the
bamboo curtain. What do the people over there want?
Some of these young Chinese well know, for they have come
out from the Red regime!

One of the staff tells how she attended a fine church in
northeast China until it was degraded to nothing less than
a political rally by the Communists. Later she moved to
another city where she got a job in an office. One noon,
while the girls were eating their lunch, someone turned on
a radio and from the speaker came the music and words of
the Christian Church. They stopped and listened! Finding
it difficult to keep from identifying herself as one who regularly listened to the program from Manila, she noticed the
others intent to catch every word. One remarked, "What
strange music and words!" Nothing was said, but they listened all the way through the broadcast.

* * * *

The Portable Missionary department with its staff of five,
under the capable directorship of Mr. Montejo, has purchased specially made pretuned flashlight-battery-powered
transistor receivers from the Philips Company in Holland.
That they are much better than the sets assembled in the
Philippines can hardly be doubted. Purchased by the hundreds, they are less expensive and come treated for the
tropics. Advent of the transistorized circuit did away with
the heavy, expensive battery pack. The remarkable stories
about the PM's could fill one complete volume!

The Cordillera Mountains separate the Cagayan River
valley of northeastern Luzon from the lowland plains of
central Luzon. All traffic from Manila to this northern area
must pass over a single road through Dalton Pass, a 35-mile
stretch of mountain road. The pass is closed after dark, and
all traffic is held up to form convoys to go through the pass

every two hours with armed Philippine constabulary escort. At the head of this pass is a café owned by an active Christian lady who holds a PM that is doubtless listened to by more different people in any one month than any other PM in service. Every bus and truck must stop at this café. Passengers are obliged to wait in the café until the convoy is ready to proceed. It would be hard to estimate how many travelers have heard the Gospel in this eating place!

The following letter came from an Igorot village:

> Besao Proper
> Besao, Mt. Province
> Philippines

DEAR FRIENDS:

We heard you here very clear and enjoyed your programs. The singing was also well understood, maybe because what we heard was not accompanied with instrumental music.

We have a radio from the Far East Broadcasting Company: they loaned it to us. We enjoy hearing the radio broadcast about the living God and His teaching.

We are Igorots living in this mountain pagan village. This is the only radio in this village of many people. No need for me to tell you what the hearers say: I have no word to describe their joys or feelings to hear a beautiful box talking.

We want to know about your teaching. Ninety eight percent of the people here worship the false god. They do not read the Bible.

We are interested to know about your doctrines and organizations.

May the good Lord bless you and your radio broadcast.

We hope to receive reply from you.

> Your hearer,
> JUAN GAWE

In the valleys of the Sierra Madre Mountains live between five and six thousand Ilongot headhunters. Why are these people killers?

1. To procure a wife. (They must present one head trophy.)
2. To settle a grudge against a neighbor.
3. To please the spirits.
4. For the sport or pleasure of killing.
5. In revenge against lowlanders who drive them from their land.

Armed with a bow and deadly sharp arrows, or a World War II Japanese rifle, and a razor-sharp bolo knife, these men take vengeance, ambush their prey, shoot without warning, and behead their victim.

Isolated from conventional means of travel and communication, the Ilongots live unto themselves. Forced probably by fear of extinction, they have become the natural enemy of the farmers who inhabit the low country at the foot of the Sierre Madre Mountains. With the desire to increase their rice production, the lowland farmers covet the fertile valleys to the east. The Ilongot headhunters have had to hold their grounds by such drastic means that it has made it extremely difficult for anyone to enter their private domain.

Confirmed in the belief that teeth are not a thing of beauty (after all, water buffalo have teeth!), both men and women go through a ceremony, in their teens, at which time the elders of the village file all the teeth near the gum and break them off. Lips and mouth are hideously reddened by chewing betel nut—a common practice of tribal people throughout Asia.

One of the Ilongot chiefs was converted to Christ through the ministry of Florentino Santos, a Filipino missionary working among the headhunters. His was not the only conversion in the small village: his family also chose to follow the Lord.

A custom among Ilongot headhunters when a wedding is about to take place is to send the young groom-to-be out to get a human head to present to his bride. Instead of sending his young son out to kill, the chief sent him to Manila to get a PM. They wanted to hear the Gospel daily! Florentino and two red-lipped Ilongot ex-headhunters stood before Mr. Montejo's desk asking for a PM for their village. Because the PM's were temporarily out of stock, he promised to take one up to them on his next PM ministering trip.

Mr. Isabelo Montejo wrote:

"Flying low between mountain peaks, we came to a clearing in the vast jungle of the great Sierra Madre Mountains somewhere between Nueva Ecija and Nueva Viscaya.

"Pilot Lee German banked the Piper Super Cub to the left and said, 'Look down there,' and right below us, standing by a grass-roofed house, was Florentino Santos. We made a perfect landing.

"The PM radio which I took attracted their attention and they came from far and near to listen to the music and messages. They were greatly fascinated by the radio and couldn't seem to understand how a small box could produce such loud music and voice!"

* * * *

The 50,000-watt transmitter in Manila was steadily sending out the Good News of salvation in the Russian language. The two letters which follow were sent from Russian listeners to the Manila office (unedited):

DEAR DIRECTOR:

Last night I overheard your broadcast directed to the Soviet Union for the first time. I believed with interest that which I heard. You mentioned that whomsoever is interested in Christian literature should send for same.

I work as an actor for a theater in Barnaola. I would love to have books from which I can obtain knowledge. Who wouldn't like to know more? I am interested in all peoples' religions, but up to now I can't comprehend why everyone's creed or confession of faith is different.

I have long desired to read the Bible—to know and learn its meaning, but have never seen or had a Bible. I borrowed a Bible commentary and read same.

If you are able I would appreciate having a Bible of my own. Please advise me by mail and not on the radio. I am willing to pay. Tell me where to send remittance.

Yours truly,
(signed) ....

Hello Friends:

We are writing to you from .... We are from the western Ukraine.

We are giving you our opinion about your broadcasts. We listen to you with eagerness and thank you from our whole heart.

We beg of you to send us God's Book because it is impossible to get it here.

Good-bye,
(signature illegible)

* * * *

The mighty voice of KSBU had been on the air for a short time. The entire staff of engineers on Okinawa and the programming personnel in Hong Kong could hardly wait until they received their first listener response letter from the mainland of China. Was the signal getting out? How far? Were the jammers at work yet?

Finally, reports started to come in by way of Hong Kong:

Dear Sir,

On October 6 at 4:45 A.M., I received your station broadcasting. You are using records produced by our mother country. This makes me very glad.

My receiving set is a battery, single tube type. At first the signal very strong, quality clear and good, and no drift of frequency observed. At about 5:30 A.M. volume gradually became small, with level going up and down, and shaky too, until nothing could be heard. Most probably this was due to the time and my receiving set having poor sensitivity.

Besides, I never heard your station before; this was the first time. You keep on saying your call letters, so you must be just beginning and testing. When you are actually getting on the air, please send me a schedule. Hope you will reply.

Pay you attention of respect.

> Yours,
> (signed) . . . .

North China

GREETINGS TO YOU AT THE GOSPEL STUDIO,

I am a mainland listener in the north, and have been hearing your testing signal quite clearly, including all contents. I am sending you the report of listening as required.

From 4:00 A.M. to 5:00 A.M. I have heard your station many times. It is very near a local station—870 kc. Quality very good. But there is some drifting from the dial setting.

Please tell me the exact frequency, location of transmitter, broadcasting time, and program schedule.

> Thank you,
> (signed) . . . .

DEAR BROTHER IN THE LORD,

Recently I bought a radio set. One day about 11:00 P.M. (Peking time) I received a preaching broadcast accidentally. The frequency is 850 kc. At least, I heard that the communicative address is P.O. Box 5966. Therefore I follow this address and write to you. I write this letter mainly for two reasons: First, I hope you will let me know the time of your broadcasts. I really hope that I can listen to it regularly. To me, after 11:00 P.M. is not very suitable. It is too late. It may affect my work next morning. I earnestly hope there may be some other time beside this. I believe some other listeners may have this need too.

For certain reasons I have forsaken meetings for several years. I am longing for the message and the preaching of the Gospel as those which I listen from the broadcasts. Usually I just read the Bible and pray at home. I don't take part in group activities. But in my heart there is a real need for fellowship with brothers and sisters. The second thing is that I hope you can send me some Gospel booklet or magazine.

Pray that the Lord may grant you grace and bless your work. Give my best regards to brothers and sisters of the Hong Kong church.

> Brother in the Lord,
> (signed) ....

Shanghai, China

Dear Radio Friends,

I am a young man. Almost every morning I listen to your religious broadcast in Cantonese. I am eager to understand the truth of Jesus but what I hear is rather piecemeal and in the local bookstores we cannot buy this type of literature. On December 3 the broadcast you said that you had a book called Youth Companion which was suitable for young folks and would answer questions about Christianity. Therefore I am writing especially to ask you for a copy. I do not know whether you can send me one. When you answer please send me a schedule of your broadcasts with the wavelengths because sometimes I cannot get your program.

> God bless you,
> (signed) ....

SIR:

When tuning to my radio I listened to the Gospel broadcasts, knowing there is a *Dengta magazine.*

But in mainland we are forbidden to subscribe this magazine. I wonder if you can send me several copies. One sent to my home address ....

But there is a request if you send me the magazine, the wrappings must be ordinary. Please do not use papers printed with—"Believe in Jesus" or "Have eternal life," etc., or any propaganda words. If it is so wrapped, please don't send it. I don't want it.

Please let me know the following address: where is the Far East Broadcasting Bible Correspondence School?

Please let me know. I want to ask them about their time of broadcasts.

Emmanuel,

(signed) ....

In the preceding letters the reader will note the requests for Bibles and other Christian literature. The Far East Broadcasting Company has had to adhere rigidly to a policy made some years ago. No letters are answered which come from Communist China. The reasons are these: Most of the individuals writing do not realize the trouble they are inviting to write such a letter to a foreign country, and especially addressed to an international radio station. To answer the letter could cause the listener untold persecution—even death. Offers for Christian literature are often made by missionaries preparing tapes for release from Manila. Perhaps the primary target area of that missionary is not China, but Chinese within the mainland hear and request the material. Occasionally, FEBC personnel in Manila will forward a request to a missionary or group who have been successful in getting such material behind the "curtains." However, some missions agree with FEBC's policy of not answering letters coming from the curtain countries. It is a known fact: accusation trials that are held against a person in China are often built around the person listening to international radio broadcasts!

Chapter Twenty-one

PROGRAMMING PROBLEMS

IN MISSIONARY BROADCASTING, the number one concern is not necessarily keeping the transmitter operating at peak capacity. Probably the most important phase of this unique ministry is what goes out over the air.

Years of experience have borne out one fact to the program producer: there must be a proper balance between religious and cultural releases. Though most broadcasters would hesitate to use the word "bait," that is what a portion of the programming really is (except KSBU, reaching China, which uses mostly religious programming).

The man who goes fishing means business. He wants to catch fish. But if he uses a shiny steel hook, he may go home without a string of fish. In broadcasting to nations of people who have been slaves to false religions for centuries, the producer is aware that the listener is probably not interested in his presentation of the Gospel of Christ. However, music is something everyone seems to love, and current news is always appreciated. With a relatively low percent of religious programming, the listener will put up with the Gospel to enjoy the other. But as the Spirit of God starts His work in collaboration with the spoken Word, he begins to see his lost condition and need of Christ.

There is a vast difference of opinion among missionary radio enthusiasts concerning the matter of programming. Some believe it is unwise to use time and money to broadcast secular music and cultural material over facilities dedicated to the propagation of the Gospel and supported by

Christians. Other international stations of many times the power of missionary radio stations spend all their time in this sort of programming. Why try to compete with them? The same insist it is the job of missionary radio to preach the Gospel without bait programs and trust the Holy Spirit to work in the hearts of potential millions to respond to the truth. Christ did not prelude his ministry with a secular concert to get a crowd. He taught them straightforwardly. Some believed—others didn't.

On the other hand, broadcasters generally feel it is hard to hold the attention of the unsaved listening audience with 100 percent Gospel programs. This is no doubt true where many hours a day are devoted to programs in the same language and area. They feel bait programs are necessary to lure the listener into hearing bits of Gospel among secular entertainment. One of the most important workers in missionary radio is the program producer. He needs divine wisdom continually in knowing what is needed in the way of effective programs for millions of potential listeners.

There are programs designed to strengthen the Christian; there are many produced for evangelistic appeal. Religious programs are given prime time. To be a service to the nations FEBC wishes to serve and to conform to the requirements of the franchise, they have tried to develop a type of programming that will reach all classes of people to accomplish the most effective job.

FEBC services feature a well rounded news program to Asia throughout the day and night. Listeners have emphasized their confidence in FEBC news, "because of the type of station you are."

Special Events Department regularly covers the activities of the president of the Philippines. The regular press conferences are covered as are his speeches to the nation. FEBC's station DZH6 is the main carrier of nationwide hookups in the Philippines. From off this frequency stations in the

Visayas and Mindanao to the south pick up messages of national significance and rebroadcast them.

"Hello Neighbor" is a program of international good will and friendship and features representatives of various nations, explaining life in their particular countries. These programs are supervised by personnel in embassies located in Manila.

Qualified educators have regularly presented lectures on various subjects through FEBC's facilities. In 1959, the first in a series of broadcasts designed for the classrooms of the Philippines was carried over the nationwide facilities of FEBC in close collaboration with the Philippine Broadcasting Service. An initial number of five hundred receiving sets donated to Philippine public schools by the Australian government and widely distributed throughout the land were a part of this project.

As part of its efforts to reach the people at the "grass roots level," FEBC's Extension Department sets up listening clubs in out-of-the-way areas of the Philippines. Approximately 1,600 clubs are now active in the Philippines. PM's have been loaned to responsible persons who report regularly to the head office in Manila. Many thousands each month receive messages of faith and freedom. There are over two thousand applications on file waiting for PM's when available. In other Asian countries there are listening posts, but not as many as in the Philippines.

* * * *

From the ashes of the disastrous fire which destroyed the facilities of KSAB and KSDX in Naha, Okinawa, emerged a new concrete office and studio building. The wife of a U.S. serviceman wrote:

> This is the first time in my life I am able to say that one of the reasons I hate to change military bases is because of a radio station. But I am going to miss KSAB

as much as I will many of my close friends here on Okinawa. Your station has helped me to grow tremendously as a Christian, and I'm sure that this is the most important thing in the world.

• • • •

The following letters received in Hong Kong prove the results of Gospel broadcasts:

> Ng Yat Fan
> Cell 5
> Government Prison
> Nung Mo Hill, Macao

DEAR BRETHREN AND SISTERS OF FAR EAST BROADCASTING STATION:

May peace of our Lord be with you. I am a person who has met with misfortune and am now serving a prison term in the prison of the Macao government. But at the same time I am also a Christian.

When I first entered this place of filth and dirt, I only felt that my surroundings were gray and unreal. Every part of my body seemed to have been bitten by poisonous snakes. I felt I loathed this world and wanted to leave it.

Thank God, He has finally saved me from the clutches of the devil. He made me understand the goal of being a human being correctly. He furthermore enabled me to understand the true meaning of life. Because of His grace, my body which is so near to death has been given a new life (John 14:6).

Though at present I am being incarcerated and have lost my freedom, I am feeling no pain because of the nearness of God. On the contrary, I am at peace and happy.

It was a moonlit midnight when my fellow cell mates were sleeping, but I was suddenly awakened by a faint voice. I rubbed my eyes and to my surprise discovered the cell mate, who slept by my side, was tuning in his transistor radio. He put the earphone in my ear without my asking, so I discovered your correspondence address. Maybe this was an inspiration from God.

Dear brethren and sisters, I give my sincere call from my heart. I hope most earnestly you will give me your help in the improvement of my soul and I shall also be most grateful if you will send me by post the Holy Bible and other spiritual food.

Finally, let's all pray together, and may peace be with you.

Yours, respectfully,
NG CHI

One month later, the following letter was received from Ng Chi:

Your letter, the Holy Bible, and books have all been received last week. I wish to express my sincere thanks. The Bible is the Treasure of Life, and the lighthouse in the ocean. I shall carefully treasure it and from the Lord's hints discover the spring of my spiritual life.

The program "Bible Drama," broadcasted by your station from 10:00 to 10:15 in the evening, has become an invaluable and indispensable enjoyment in my life after listening to it for many nights. Its taste is like honey. It can stimulate people who are dispirited, and make unhappy people happy. To those of you, brothers and sisters, who work for the Lord, this is praiseworthy. May the Lord's grace be with you forever.

Yours in Christ,
NG CHI

A letter written in Chinese came from an Indonesian listener:

DEAR SIRS:

Several months ago your station announced that the Lord Jesus had already come to earth. Please, may I ask, where is Jesus now? Will you please tell me? Later, your station said that this was the time of the Lord's judgment. Please, may I ask, where is the Lord judging the sinful human race? True, the human race has already reached the limit of its sinfulness. Such things as the war in China, the Dutch-Indonesian war, the war in Viet Nam, and other such conflicts, plus the development of the atom and hydrogen bombs—all these things show that human sinfulness is reaching its final stage. So if the world has a Saviour who has come to serve the human race, I feel I would most surely want to welcome Him. So, I am asking your station to inform me as to the whereabouts of His headquarters.

Chapter Twenty-two

MIRACLE STATION

DURING THE DARK DAYS of World War II, General MacArthur announced to the people of the Philippine Islands the famous words, "I shall return!" One of the four Voice of Freedom stations operated by the Office of War Information which carried these well-known words was KGEI, located in the San Francisco Bay area. Originally built by General Electric Corporation for a display at the World's Fair in 1939, many thousands of people viewed with awe this powerful transmitter broadcasting to foreign lands. After the fair was concluded, the equipment was moved to its permanent location on the salt flats near Belmont, California.

About that time it was taken over by the Office of War Information and used during the war years to broadcast encouragement and hope to the Filipinos under Japanese occupation.

After the war ended, General Electric again took it over and, in cooperation with Stanford University, used the station as an eductaional project reaching Latin America, during those years building up a high-class listening audience.

A group of Christian businessmen from Detroit bought KGEI and operated it as an international broadcasting station with some Christian programming for one and a half years. Don Smith, who had worked with FEBC in Manila, was engineer.

When Don learned they wanted to sell it, and especially to a Christian group, he called the home office in Whittier, but the response was weak—they were not interested. With

two hot irons in the fire (Manila and Okinawa with the
50,000-watt and 100,000-watt stations), they didn't feel they
dared tackle another major project right then.

"But I think you should at least come up and look at it,"
Don insisted.

"Well, we'll be up tomorrow and look it over, but I don't
think we can get excited about it," Bob Bowman returned.

While viewing the 50,000-watt shortwave transmitter located in a two-story reinforced concrete building, and the
antenna array, the directors of FEBC became aware of the
potential before them—a shortwave station and an audience
already listening!

As the men drove away from KGEI, one of them looked
back and said, "You know, the property alone is worth the
price they are asking." Several of the other men were dis-
cussing the problem of raising the downpayment—$27,000.00.
Worst of all, they had only twenty-four hours to make up
their minds.

After returning to the home office, they spent some time
in prayer and committed the whole matter to the Lord. After
all, they had little money in the bank, and both other projects were demanding heavy expenditures in the near future.

Within nineteen hours $27,000.00 came in from three
different sources! One was a legacy which they knew about
but didn't expect to receive for two years because of some
legal proceedings. This was the exact amount the Detroit
men had asked for the downpayment.

The FCC license was received in February, 1960, and they
went on the air as a Far East Broadcasting station March
27, 1960. But that is not the end of the miracles.

It is one thing to own a station and have a license, but it
is quite another thing to have a staff to operate it. Richard
Bronson* became general director. Don Smith was the

_____
*The FEBC Board of Directors was increased to five members with
Richard Bronson and Robert Reynolds added.

only member of the staff when FEBC took over. But at that time a young man, Carl Lawrence, who had worked his way up to a high salary in C.B.S. television in Hollywood but was dissatisfied with that kind of life, was led to contact FEBC's home office. After knowing the salary he had been receiving, they were almost ashamed to say what his allowance would be if he went to work for FEBC as station manager of KGEI! But he accepted it.

Lillian Russell had worked for twenty-eight years as secretary and bookkeeper for a large paint company in Spokane, Washington. She had reached the age of retirement but didn't want to retire! Offering her services to KGEI as a secretary, she filled a much needed position.

Clyde Hull, who had been so helpful in getting the big giant on the air in Manila, came to the rescue as another engineer. The Lord sent in other staff members as needs arose.

Since the transmitter had been built thirty-one years before, it was using an old-type power tube that cost $835.00 (two were required). One afternoon, Don Smith and several other KGEI personnel stopped by a large international broadcasting station. (The same group had been in the habit of giving the engineers in Manila tubes after they had run their expected life. Many times a tube will operate hundreds of hours after its rated life is completed. But, because of policy, the other organization removed such tubes and replaced them with new ones.) Don asked if they had any expired tubes, but there were none available, nor would there be any for months. As they were leaving the building, Don happened to pass by a trash can where papers and sweepings were placed. On the top of the can lay a big power tube exactly like the type KGEI used. Don asked, "What are you going to do with this tube?"

"It's no good—filament is broken. We're throwing it away."

Probably having in mind a unique use for the tube, Don

asked if he could have it. (After all, most people never saw a large power tube. It would make a good display in missionary conferences.) "Sure. Take it. It's no good to us."

Some time later, Clyde Hull was making some tests on the 50,000-watt transmitter during off-the-air time in the morning. He had just pushed the main switch when a meter indicated one of the main tubes had burned out. Being alone and a bit frustrated at the situation, he ran downstairs to get a spare, only to find the new spare had not yet arrived. He was stunned!

Over on the work bench lay the tube which had been taken out of the trash can. It was covered with a layer of dust and, as the engineer said, was worthless because of a broken filament.

Hull grabbed the tube, dusted it off, and carried it up to the rear of the transmitter, not really knowing why he did it. After installing it in the complicated socket, he threw the main switch; but as he expected, nothing happened. The rest of the transmitter hummed with power, but the needle on the meter indicating how much power that tube was putting out was pointing to zero! Just then the phone rang, and being alone in the building, Hull went to the office to answer. After a brief conversation he returned, and to his utter astonishment, the meter indicated the tube was putting out full power! The filament had welded itself together.

Describing this to the staff later, Hull said, "There was a feeling as if it were holy! I was startled! Theoretically, it couldn't happen. I felt like Moses—standing on holy ground."

God met the need. He didn't provide a new tube when it was needed but chose to produce a miracle in restoring usefulness to a damaged one. That tube served faithfully for eleven months!

In the meantime, engineers were busy in the basement, building a unit that would modify and modernize a section of the transmitter. It would use a new type of tube that is 40 percent more effective, takes less power, and costs $200.00 less. It took months to complete the modification, which moved along as the Lord provided the means. Then, the day arrived when all hands were standing by to help in the changeover. The plans were that as soon as the power was shut off after sign-off, all would work through the night. The section of the transmitter that was to be replaced would be taken out and the new unit installed. If everything went well, they would be on the air the next day without any loss of time.

Tools were close by; the new unit was on the floor near the transmitter. The announcer gave the sign-off and the national anthem was played—but as the last notes were sounding out, the "miracle" tube died, and the transmitter automatically kicked off the air!

By sign-on time the next afternoon, the transmitter had been tested and was ready to go on the air with new modern power tubes!

* * * *

Letters of encouragement arrived from different Latin American countries. A survey of such letters indicated 60 percent were typewritten, showing a more highly educated class of listeners. Letters often come from students, professors, insurance agents, factory executives, office workers, farmers, military personnel, radio men, miners, druggists, bankers, doctors, railroad agents and high school principals.

From Ecuador came a letter of special note:

It will not be very easy for you to imagine the amount of pleasure that comes to me through the medium of your everyday broadcasting reports.

All of the varied sections of the programs you are broadcasting are worthy of special attention; but those that produce a quivering sensation within me are the religious ones. Why so? It is just because the tunes of many of the songs or hymns sung in the programs are very familiar to me. When a youngster in my native land, British Guiana, I have had the pleasure of singing them myself at Sunday school on repeated occasions; hence, you may easily judge the kind of emotional feelings that assault me upon hearing them sung in a chorus as in former days. Now, I am an aged man past 80 years old, living far away from my original home.

Despiting that, however, it is also pleasing to know that your friendly communications night after night, in addition to the never-failing presence of God are nearby.

Therefore, may God bless and protect you in order you may be allowed to continue for a lengthened period of time broadcasting His precious Word, in addition to the topics that are included in your friendly programs for the benefit of your fellow men.

I am also deeply interested in the story of Communism you lecture upon so often. I therefore kindly implore you to grant me a copy of *El Corazón del Communism* offered by you in your talks.

A captain of an airliner wrote KGEI the following letter:

Buenos Aires, Argentina

DEAR SIRS:

While we were flying from Sao Paulo, Brazil to Buenos Aires, by some rare chance we turned on our shortwave radio to alleviate a bit of tension that we were feeling since we were flying through the middle of a powerful and dangerous storm.

Suddenly, the voice of the announcer broke through loud and clear with a quote from the Bible, which to both of us resulted as a ray of light in the obscurity of the atmosphere. It was a firm promise, an assurance that I have never experienced during all the years I have been flying. Now I wouldn't want to be caught guilty

of exaggeration nor of hypersensibility; but the fact is
that it seemed to us that the very presence of the Eternal
was vibrating in our beings, saying to us, "Fear not, you
will arrive without harm . . . am I not traveling with
you?"

The odd thing is *both* of us thought the same thing
and at the same time, and felt that sensation of security.
Something was there. It wasn't just sensory. It was
something profound, unexplainable, yet so sure, that it
was worthy of credit as the inevitable daily setting of
the sun.

It would seem to me to be some sort of announcement
from God, since I have left the Way. I stopped believing in God in 1944 as I was about to cut the throat of a
German paratrooper in Italy, in the midst of a beautiful
little chestnut forest beneath an entrancing moon. How
great an error! There exists a something—a Power that
rules the heavens and earth.

To sum it up, the feeling that we now have is not one
of just thankfulness for having been delivered from danger, but one of comfort. It's as though suddenly we had
an assurance, a new force. Could you perhaps explain
to me better this phenomenon?

Chapter Twenty-three

URGENCY

BECAUSE OF THE ADVENTURES of Marco Polo and the tales of the Arabian Nights, the Far East and Asia have fascinated adventurers from every quarter of the globe. The picturesque sights and exotic sounds are not the true picture of the Eastern world.

Far beyond the Japanese torii and its Shinto shrine lies disappointment. The Indian returns from his temple worship disillusioned, carrying the same load of sin back home with him. God has created man for Himself, and the human heart is restless until it finds its rest in Him.

Inside the gorgeous temples of Japan, Thailand, and India is deceit, for:

> The idols of the heathen are silver and gold, the work of men's hands.
> They have mouths, but they speak not; eyes have they, but they see not;
> They have ears, but they hear not; neither is there any breath in their mouths.
> They that make them are like unto them: so is every one that trusteth in them.
> — Ps. 135:15-18.

Following the glowing promises of Communism comes disillusionment, for proletarian "classless" rule has not solved the problems of inequality, injustice, and poverty.

Asia—lands of lotus blossom and sandalwood, pagoda and rickshaw, temples and teeming millions, but also lands of disappointment, disillusionment and stark, wretched soul need.

"Whosoever shall call upon the name of the Lord shall be saved"—but how shall the people of Asia call on One of whom they have never heard? How shall they hear without a preacher?

Thank God, there have been messengers. From the days of Adoniram Judson and Robert Morrison, Hudson Taylor and Jonathan Goforth, through to the present day, there have been messengers—but far too few.

God has raised up an air force to supplement the work of the gallant infantrymen in the missionary army. That air force is missionary radio.

FEBC's fifteen transmitters, using seventeen frequencies, sound forth the Gospel message in thirty-six languages, 758½ hours per week. FEBC's monthly operating budget, including missionary allowances, has soared to $43,000.00!

Those who have enrolled in the Bible Correspondence School of the Air, Manila, total 700,000 (not counting courses offered from other missions or stations) with 2,000 new enrollees a week.

One is reminded of the urgency in getting out an important message in the days of Queen Esther. A people had been sentenced to death because of the wickedness of Haman. His hatred for Mordecai, the gatekeeper, enraged him to the point of plotting the scheme to have the entire Jewish race wiped out.

The message signed by the king had been sent to all one hundred twenty-seven provinces, proclaiming that the Jews should be killed on a certain day.

After the death sentence had gone forth, sealed by the king's ring, it was discovered that Haman had planned this for his own self-gratification. Haman was hanged on the gallows he had prepared for the hated gatekeeper, Mordecai.

The sentence of death had been delivered! According to law, not even the king could reverse his orders. The only thing to do now was to send out new messages to the one hundred twenty-seven provinces, giving instructions to the Jews that they were permitted to fight for their lives.

The new orders, "messages of life," were written in the king's name and sealed with the king's seal. These important orders were copied in the languages of the people so there would be no misunderstanding.

The area, covering a vast part of the Middle East, was to be flooded with these important letters from the king. Every fast means available was used: riders on horseback, mules, camels, and young dromedaries sped across the burning desert and over the barren mountains.

Then, the Word of God tells us, the riders went out, "being hastened and pressed on by the king's commandment."

Today, if this happened, radio would be the means of getting such an important message out to the masses of people.

But, we do not need to say, "If this happened." It is happening! Men and women the world over are condemned to death. The sentence has been pronounced upon them! The only way they can be freed is to receive the important "message of life."

We have the message—we have the means. The commandment has been given! "Go ye into all the world, and preach the gospel to every creature."

How gratifying to know the orders of King Ahasuerus were carried out implicitly. The messages arrived on time. No life was lost. The Jews had joy and gladness.

But not so with the millions of the world today. We have not taken the command from the King of kings as seriously as they did in King Ahasuerus' day. If we would take up the challenge, radio could be the means whereby the Gospel could be preached to every creature. In perfect teamwork with missionaries, radio can be used where men are forbidden.

Dipping into hidden valleys; circling thousands of isolated islands; sweeping up inaccessible mountains; penetrating curtain barriers; invading the privacy of the guarded home; finding an open heart in the lonely byways or in the teeming cities—here and there the Gospel light touches a heart, and it bursts into flame to light a home or to fire a community. This is MISSIONARY RADIO—a ministry the Far East Broadcasting Company is dedicated to perform.

For further information concerning the activities of FEBC,
write to:

Far East Broadcasting Company
Box 1
Whittier, California